A DORSET SOLDIER

In the Spellmount/Nutshell Military list:

The Territorial Battalions - A pictorial history
The Yeomanry Regiments - A pictorial history
Over the Rhine - The Last Days of War in Europe
History of the Cambridge University OTC
Yeoman Service
Intelligence Officer in the Peninsula
The Scottish Regiments - A pictorial history
The Royal Marines - A pictorial history
The Royal Tank Regiment - A pictorial history
The Irish Regiments - A pictorial history
British Sieges of the Peninsular War
Victoria's Victories
Heaven and Hell: German Paratroop war diary
Rorke's Drift
The Fighting Troops of the Austro-Hungarian Army
Came the Dawn - Fifty years an Army Officer
Kitchener's Army - A pictorial history
On the Word of Command - A pictorial history of the Regimental Sergeant Major
Marlborough as Military Commander
The Art of Warfare in the Age of Marlborough
Epilogue in Burma 1945-48
Scandinavian Misadventure
The Fall of France
The First Victory: O'Connor's Desert Triumph,Dec 1940-Feb 1941
Blitz Over Britain
Deceivers Ever - Memoirs of a Camouflage Officer
Indian Army of the Empress 1861-1903
Heroes for Victoria 1837-1901
The Waters of Oblivion - the British Invasion of the Rio de la Plata, 1806-07.
Soldier's Glory - 'Rough Notes of an Old Soldier'
Craufurd's Light Division
Napoleon's Military Machine
Falklands Military Machine
Wellington's Military Machine
Commando Diary
The French are Coming! The Invasion Scare 1803-05
Military Marching - A pictorial history
Soldier On! - Testament of a Tom
The Glider Soldiers
Sons of John Company - The Indian and Pakistan Armies, 1903-91
A Guards Officer in the Peninsula
Gentlemen's Sons: The Guards in the Peninsula and at Waterloo
Unforgettable Army

In the Nautical List:

Evolution of Engineering in the Royal Navy, Vol 1. 1827-1939
In Perilous Seas
Sea of Memories

In the Aviation List:

Diary of a Bomb Aimer
Operation 'Bograt' - Memoirs of a Fighter Pilot
A Medal for Life-Capt Leefe Robinson VC
Three Decades a Pilot-The Third Generation
Bob Doe - Fighter Pilot
The Allied Bomber War, 1939-45

A DORSET SOLDIER

The Autobiography of Sergeant William Lawrence

Edited by Eileen Hathaway

SPELLMOUNT LTD
Tunbridge Wells

© Eileen Hathaway 1993
ISBN 1-873376-05-7

First published in the UK by
SPELLMOUNT LTD
12 Dene Way
Speldhurst
Tunbridge Wells
Kent
TN3 0NX

A catalogue record for this book is available from the British Library

Printed in Great Britain by
BIDDLES LTD
Woodbridge Park
Guildford
Surrey

TABLE OF CONTENTS

ILLUSTRATIONS

1. The Storming of Monte Video, February 3rd 1807. British troops move forward in the darkness to storm the breach in the town's walls.

2. The death of Captain Renny of the 40th Regiment. Renny was shot dead as he reached the top of the breach at Monte Video.

3. The Battle of Talavera, July 27th-28th 1809.

4. The Battle of Bussaco, September 27th 1810. Marshal Reynier's attack upon that part of the Allied line held by the British 3rd Division.

5. Allied troops file into the Lines of Torres Vedras in late autumn of 1810.

6. The British Army fording the Mondego river in pursuit of Massena's army in the spring of 1811.

7. 'Saving the Colour at the Battle of Albuera, May 16th 1811.' The 3rd Regiment (The Buffs) fight to hold off Polish lancers during the battle.

8. 'A View of the Siege and Storming of Ciudad Rodrigo in Spain on January 19th 1812'. An old print showing the storming of the town.

9. 'Badajos on the Guadiana, as approached from Albuquerque and Elvas'. The town as seen from the left bank. On the extreme left can be seen the high walls of the castle.

10. 'Badajos Taken by Storm on the 6th of April 1812 by the Allied Army under Lord Wellington'. British troops move forward to storm the breaches at Badajoz.

11. Wellington inspects the breaches at Badajoz on the morning of April 7th 1812 following the successful but appalling and bloody storming of the place the previous night.

12. The centre of the British Army at the Battle of Waterloo, June 18th 1815. British infantry squares under attack from French cavalry close to La Haye Sainte.

13. The Battle of Waterloo. Wellington encourages the hard-pressed British infantry squares as French cavalry approach.

14. An Officer and Private of the 40th Regiment of Foot, 1815.

15. William Lawrence's grave at St Nicholas' churchyard, Studland.

16. Studland, about 1888. The building on the right is the 'New' inn, now the Bankes' Arms. The cottage on the left was the 'Old' inn, ie Lawrence's 'Wellington Inn'. (*Dorset County Museum*)

17. George Bankes' Manor House, now the Manor Hotel, Studland.

MAPS

ACKNOWLEDGEMENTS

I would like to thank everyone who has helped with my research into William Lawrence's life: the staff at the Dorset County Record Office, the Dorset County Museum and Library Service, and the Public Record Office in Kew; Mrs Elizabeth Deverell for her grandmother's reminiscence of William Lawrence; Mrs Pauline Ferguson for access to the information on Lawrence compiled by her husband, Colonel Kenneth Ferguson DSO, TD, DL; to Kay Harlow, Margaret Lamont and Dawn Waring for their positive comments and useful criticism of the manuscript; to Major General S C Grant for his foreword; and to Anthony Mitchell of the National Trust who was so helpful with queries relating to the Bankes Family of Kingston Lacy. Particular thanks go to Lt-Col (Rtd) E G Bostock, Curator of the Queen's Lancashire Regiment Museum, for his patience with my queries, his assistance in tracing archive material, and for allowing me to include illustrations of the uniforms worn in 1804, 1814 and 1815 by the men of the 40th Regiment.

Thanks are also due to Ian Fletcher for his help, and to Dawn Waring for the knowledge and skill that enabled her to create an image of Lawrence in his grenadier's uniform. That portrait now graces the cover of this book.

The letters about Thomas Linnington's apprenticeship are part of the Frampton Estate archives housed at the County Record Office, Dorchester, and are reproduced here with their kind permission. The period photograph of Studland is included with the permission of the Dorset County Museum.

FOREWORD

by

MAJOR GENERAL S. C. GRANT

Colonel of the Queen's Lancashire Regiment

Doctor Johnson suggested that 'every man thinks meanly of himself for not having been a soldier, or not having been to sea'. However, most men in Britain under the age of 50 have never served in the Army and, as a result, they have never experienced the fears and horrors of war, nor the hardships and intense loyalties inextricably linked with military service. To such readers, William Lawrence's autobiography, with its simple, vivid descriptions of the campaigns of the 40th Regiment some 200 years ago, provides, like Stephen Crane's classic novel *The Red Badge of Courage*, sharp insights into the nature of war - insights made all the more striking by the contrast that Lawrence, perhaps unwittingly, draws between the violence of the Napoleonic battlefield and the rural tranquility of nineteenth century England.

Despite the fact that Lawrence 'had no opportunity for education', no one, after reading his description of the Battle of Talavera, could fail to understand, on one hand, the cruelty of the battlefield, and, on the other, the camaraderie that exists between all soldiers. At Talavera, in a single day, approximately 12,000 soldiers were either killed or wounded; at the end of the battle 'the long grass in which the wounded were lying caught fire and many who should have been conveyed to hospital in Talavera were scorched to death'. And yet, in the middle of this violent battle, a truce was arranged to allow both sides to collect their wounded, and in a scene similar to that which would occur in the First World War on Christmas Day in 1914, the opposing soldiers came together and a 'friendly exchange sprang up between them'. Although they may, at first sight, seem strange bedfellows, savagery and compassion are never far from William Lawrence's story - nor, indeed, are they ever far from war.

In addition to making an invaluable contribution to our general understanding of warfare, William Lawrence's memoirs provide, to the military historian and the serving officer, vital background information on two other important issues; first, on Wellington's abilities as a commander; and secondly, on courage on the battlefield. Lawrence's account of service under Wellington, and particularly his description of the defence of Torres Vedras, confirms the wisdom of Field Marshal Montgomery's dictum that 'the best way to achieve high morale in war-time is by success in battle. The good general is the one who wins his battles with the fewest possible casualties'. Wellington's mastery of his profession - and of the enemy - was such that William Lawrence, a lowly foot soldier in the 40th regiment, was able to say that Wellington 'seemed to understand every move they (ie the French) made and was always ready to receive them'.

William Lawrence was a brave man. However, in his autobiography he makes no attempt to disguise the fears that he felt at various times during his time as a soldier. In the middle of the Battle of Waterloo, Lawrence was ordered to the colours - a task fraught with danger as during that day 'fourteen sergeants, and officers in proportion, had been killed or wounded in the duty'. Lawrence states that 'this was one job I did not like at all. Nevertheless, I went to work as boldly as I could'! To all serving soldiers - and particularly to the soldiers of the Queen's Lancashire Regiment, who have the honour to be the direct descendants of the gallant men of the 40th Regiment - William Lawrence has a vital message: all soldiers, with discipline and the support of their comrades in arms, have the capacity to be brave.

INTRODUCTION

In about 1857, in the Dorset coastal village of Studland, a man in his late sixties started dictating his reminiscences. As the local innkeeper he had entertained neighbours and customers alike with anecdotes from his youth, stories of when he was a soldier campaigning with the Duke of Wellington. When he retired, he was urged to write the stories down. As the old man was illiterate, a friend offered to be his amanuensis and the task was begun. How long it took to complete is not known, but when the old man died he bequeathed the manuscript to the descendants of George Bankes, a local landowner and MP. The old man's name was William Lawrence, and the manuscript - edited by Bankes' grandson, George Nugent Bankes - was published in 1886 as the 'Autobiography of Sergeant William Lawrence'.

William Lawrence served as a soldier from 1805-1821 and was present at the bloodiest and most famous actions of the Napoleonic wars. He was a participant in the maverick campaign against the Spanish in South America 1806-1807, fought in Spain, Portugal and France throughout the Peninsular War 1808-1814, and accompanied an expedition to New Orleans in North America in 1814-1815. A survivor of the infantry squares at the battle of Waterloo, he, unlike so many of his comrades, returned to Britain an able-bodied man. So mentally active was he that, in old age, he was able to recall the scenes of his youth with accuracy and humour. His story is a vivid, personal perspective of events which, for most of us today, are nothing but dates on a history chart. It is that story which is told on the pages of this book.

Until now the only copies of his autobiography have been those which have survived from 1886, 450 facsimile copies (1987), and a French translation (1897). All are so scarce that, apart from military historians and enthusiasts, most people today are ignorant of Lawrence, and of his story. His obscurity is undeserved and this publication has been devised to remedy the situation.

Why is a new edition needed? The reasons are many. To begin with, over 100 years separate modern readers from the original publication. Also, the 1886 edition was painfully bare. It contained no illustrations or maps, and the narrative - unsupported by editorial notes on either the historical or military context - could, in parts, be difficult to comprehend without specialist knowledge. The chapter introductions and footnotes in this edition contain the information needed to bridge those gaps and give the reader a smooth passage from beginning to end. Derived from original sources unavailable to Bankes in 1886, the new material builds on the factual content of Lawrence's autobiography.

George Nugent Bankes, in preparing William Lawrence's story for publication for the first time, faced many problems. The most fundamental was that the manuscript was the verbatim account of a man whose only effective means of communication was the *spoken* word. Bankes recognised that deletions and alterations were needed, but as he was having trouble enough just deciphering and punctuating the text, he shrank from the task. "If the pruning-hook had once been introduced," he explained in his Preface, "it would have been difficult to decide what to leave and what to take," so he left in everything.

In many ways this was a commendable decision, particularly as Bankes appears to have had neither the specialist knowledge, nor the research capability, to condense the narrative effectively. With the archive material available today, it is less easy for an editor to justify that decision. I have therefore decided to take to the text the 'pruning hook' Bankes chose not to use.

Nothing has been added to Lawrence's account; facts acquired through research appear either as footnotes, chapter introductions, or in the appendix. The names of places have been modernised, eg Pamplona for Pampeluna, Briantspuddle for Bryant's Piddle, but most are identifiable in modern atlases and road maps no matter what form is used.

As an autobiography, Lawrence's narrative was incomplete because it covered in detail only the years between 1804 and 1821. When finally discharged from the army, he was only 30 years old and had another 40 years to live before 'writing' his autobiography, but to those 40 years he devoted only a few paragraphs. What did he do in that time? A biographical appendix addresses this question.

Reading his autobiography you may be tempted to divorce William Lawrence the soldier from William Lawrence the civilian. The temptation should be resisted. Lawrence's experiences as a young boy were typical of those who enlisted, therefore the composition of the 40th Regiment (and other infantry regiments), and its disciplines, reflect society in Britain in the early 19th century.

It should be remembered that young William was a contemporary of novelist Jane Austen (1775-1817) and that the Peninsular War was taking place while she was in Hampshire writing her novels. In 1811, having heard news of a particularly bloody battle, she wrote from Chawton Cottage to her sister Cassandra: "How horrible it is to have so many people killed, and what a blessing one cares for none of them." William Lawrence could not write like Jane Austen, and the tales he tells are very different, but in telling them he gives us the opportunity not just to learn about some of those who fought and were killed, but to care about them too.

Eileen Hathaway
March 1993

- CHAPTER 1 -

Farm Labourer and Apprentice
1790 - 1804

As I have been asked to furnish a complete account of my life, I will start at the beginning.

I was born in 1791[1] in Briantspuddle[2], Dorset, to parents of humble means. My father had been a small farmer in the same village but, having a large and hungry family to provide for, became reduced in circumstances, and gave up his farm to work as a labourer instead[3].

One of seven children[4], I was compelled to earn my own livelihood at a very early age so I had no opportunity for education. It was no hardship for I preferred an open-air life. For some time I was paid two pence a day to frighten the birds off the corn, then I became a ploughboy and received sixpence a day. When I was fourteen, my father obtained £20 from a friend, with which he apprenticed me for seven years to Henry Bush, a builder living at Studland, also in Dorset. I was to receive no wages, but my master was to supply me with food, lodging, and clothes[5].

Things went on smoothly while the money for my apprenticeship lasted, but after a month Henry Bush became rather difficult to please. He also started rationing my food, which was a more serious matter. I put up with it for about nine months then, one Sunday, after going to church in the morning, I stayed in the village all day. When I returned home it was after dark and I found the house locked up. I went to Swanage - the nearest town - and called on my master's sister, who lived there. She took me in, and was giving me some supper, when my master came in. He was very angry with me. He told me to come along with him, declaring he would 'pay me out' in the morning.

When we got home he told me to go and see if the garden gate was shut. This was strange because I had never been asked to do so before. In the morning I understood why for he produced the horsewhip he had slipped upstairs while I had been occupied seeing to the gate. Before I had a chance to get my clothes on, he gave me a good thrashing with it. I bundled downstairs and got out of the house as quick as I could. "That's the last thrashing you give me," I said to myself. I decided to leave.

That week I and another apprentice[6] - one in similar circumstances - planned our departure. We chose a Sunday because we would be able to get away without our employers' knowing and therefore get a few hours start. We met early in the morning. Neither of us had either money or food and, as I wanted to get hold of my apprenticeship indentures, we waited until the Bush family had left to go to Swanage to chapel, so I could search the house. I entered by the back door, which was fastened by a piece of rope-yarn. I could not find my indentures[7], but I did come upon a seven-shilling piece, which I pocketed. In the chimney corner hung a flitch of bacon, marked to ensure I ate no more than my allowance. I cut off about three or four pounds, took what else I thought we should require, put it all into a bag with some bread, and left.

My companion and I went to a place nearby called King's Wood[8] where, being hungry, we ate some of our bacon and bread before walking the 10 miles to Wareham. There we changed our seven-shilling piece and had a pint of small beer[9]. After an hour's rest we carried on.

Our destination was Poole, about nine miles further on. Although very tired, we kept going. We did not reach Poole until a very late hour, so we had trouble obtaining a lodging for the rest of the night. At last, we found one in a public house, where we finished our bread and bacon, and had some more beer. It was the best day's allowance we had had for a long time.

We slept soundly, and in the morning went around inquiring for service on board the Newfoundland packets[10]. A merchant by the name of Slade agreed to hire us for two summers and a winter for which I was to be paid £20, and my companion £18, with the merchant paying for our food and lodging till the ship left the harbour.

The next day I worked on board the ship, but in the evening I fell in with the mate who asked me where I was going. I knew by his manner that something was wrong.

"To my lodgings," I said nervously.

He told me to accompany him, and I found myself confronted by my companion's master, who had come to Poole in search of us. He had met his apprentice wandering about the market, and had taken him into custody. Asked if he had seen me, the boy said I was in Poole, but he didn't know where. The master found me anyway and had me put in gaol for the night.

We were to be taken back so, next day, we were put on the Swanage market-boat. It reached South Deep near Brownsea Castle where, because the wind was contrary, it had to anchor. A number of stone-boats were also lying there[11] and one of the boatmen, Reuben Masters, who was going by my master's house, offered to take me home. We landed, he took charge of me, and we set off. About half a mile from home, we met my mistress[12] who wanted to know where I had been. She said her husband would have nothing more to do with me, and was going to send me to prison instead. I had no intention of troubling him but I did not tell her that. At the next gate, I saw my opportunity to bolt and took it. I jumped over the gate and ran away.

"You may go!" I heard Reuben Masters say. "Let your master run after you himself!"

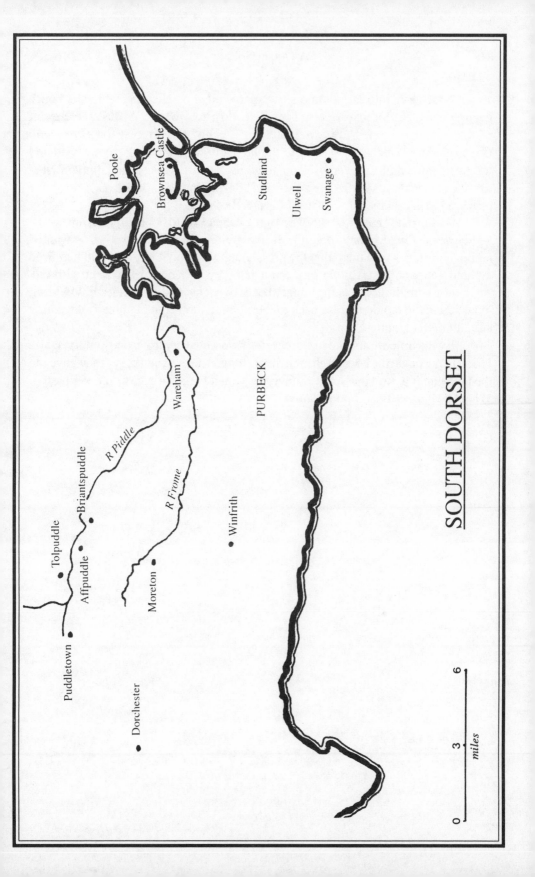

SOUTH DORSET

Poole

Brownsea Castle

Studland

Ulwell

Swanage

PURBECK

Wareham

R Piddle

Tolpuddle

Briantspuddle

Affpuddle

R Frome

Winfrith

Puddletown

Moreton

Dorchester

0   3   6
    miles

I ran down into the common, to a place called Agglestone, which had once been a great place for foxes. There I crawled into a hole to hide. At dusk, I came out of my den, and headed towards Wareham. I called this time at the *Horse and Groom*[13] where I related my story to the landlady, who kindly gave me food and lodging for the night. She advised me to go back to my parents and tell them what my master had done so, after breakfast, and after accepting the bread and cheese she provided to eat on the way, I set off for Dorchester.

On the road I met two boys who were on their way to Poole to get a ship bound for Newfoundland. They weren't fit for sailors or soldiers so, as I wanted companionship, I told them that the press-gang were about in Poole and had fired a blunderbuss at me. That alarmed them and they turned back and kept with me. They soon complained of being hungry but as they only had a shilling and a farthing to last them the hundred miles back to their home, I took out my bread and cheese and divided it amongst us.

By the time we arrived in Dorchester[14] we were very tired, and hungry again. I tried to persuade the boys to change the shilling. They wouldn't, but they gave me the farthing. It wasn't much for a hungry boy but it bought a cake to eat. We parted. What became of them, I don't know.

- CHAPTER 2 -

Fugitive and Recruit
1804 - 1806

Dorchester was only eight miles from my parents' house, but I never seriously thought of going to them. Unable to make up my mind what to do, or where to go, I ambled through the town watching the preparations for the fair, which was to take place the next day. I wandered into the stable-yard of one of the principal inns and was brought to my senses when a voice sang out: "Hey you! What do you want!"

It was the ostler. I told him I was hungry but had no money, and was in search of employment. He said if I brushed about a bit and helped him rub down the horses, he would find me plenty to eat. I did so and, sure enough, he brought me a lump of bread and beef, enough for two or three meals. I ate as much as I wanted. Afterwards I felt tired. I made up a bed with some straw and, putting the remainder of my meal into my handkerchief to serve as a pillow, I lay down. The ostler had given me a rug and this I pulled over me. I slept soundly all night.

In the morning I did some more work in the stable, then walked out into the street with my new friend. We saw some soldiers and I said I wanted to be a soldier too. The ostler knew where he could enlist me and took me straight to the rendezvous which was a public-house. Inside was a sergeant of artillery, who gave him two guineas for bringing me and myself five for coming. My measurements were taken - which caused a lot of amusement - and I was put into an old soldier's coat. With three or four yards of ribbon hanging from my cap, I paraded around town with the other recruits, entering almost every public-house, treating someone or other.

In the very first inn sat a Briantspuddle farmer, a man I knew well. He exclaimed in surprise at seeing me. I begged him not to tell my father and mother where I was, and how he had seen me, and hurried out. Then later in the day I encountered my father's next-door neighbour. He recognized me immediately. I offered him the price of a gallon of ale not to say anything to my parents. He took the money and promised he wouldn't. How I spent the rest of the night can better be imagined than described, but the next morning, I had to be sworn in at the Town Hall. I was on my way there with an officer when who should meet us but my father and mother. As soon as the neighbour had got home, he had gone and told them what I was up to. They told the officer I was an apprentice, and he gave me up to them without any trouble[1], but he asked me what had become of the bounty of five guineas. Discovering that I had only seventeen shillings and sixpence left, he kindly relieved me of even that.

My parents marched me off home, and my father went to see a magistrate[2] to find out what he should do about me. The magistrate advised him to take me back to Dorchester to be tried at the next sitting. This my father did and I was severely reprimanded by the bench. They gave me the choice of serving my time as an apprentice or going to prison[3]. Of course, I chose the former, so they gave me a letter to give to Henry Bush.

When I got downstairs, the officer was there. He said that if my master was unwilling to take me back, he would enlist me again. He asked if I had any money. I didn't, so he gave me a shilling and wished me well.

My father sent me off from Dorchester immediately, giving me strict orders to get back to Studland as quickly as I could. I received no blessing, or anything else so, with a heavy heart, I set off. I hadn't gone far when I was overtaken by a dairy cart. The dairy-man offered me a lift and I accepted. He asked where I was going. I told him some of my story and showed him the letter, getting him to open it so that I could find out what was inside. He said my master would not be able to hurt me, that it was safe to go back to Studland. That was cheering, but I didn't intend to go back anyway.

I rode with the man as far as he went, then continued on foot to a village called Winfrith. Being hungry I went into a public-house and ordered some bread and cheese. A soldier was there and the sight of him revived my spirit, and my longing to be like him. I got into conversation with him and discovered that he was on furlough, bound for Bridport. I said I wanted to be a soldier too. Straight away he said that he could enlist me in the 40th Regiment of Foot which gave 16 guineas bounty. It sounded a great deal of money. I thought that if I got hold of it I would not want for money for a long time, so I accepted his proposal without hesitation.

We headed for Bridport but, afraid of finding myself in Dorchester again, I tried to persuade the soldier to go around it. He wouldn't, but we slipped through at night, safely reaching Winterborne, where we put up.

Next morning we got the coach to Bridport and when we arrived, the coachman surprised me by remarking that it was only yesterday that my father had got me out of the artillery! He meant well but, of course, the soldier then asked me if I was an apprentice and I had no choice but to admit I was. He promptly made me get down. He took me across some fields to his home and there kept me quietly for three days.

As the barracks of the 40th Regiment were in Taunton, Somersetshire, it was there we thought it best to go. We went to see the colonel and the soldier told him that I was a recruit. The colonel asked me what trade I was in.

"I'm a labourer," I replied.

"Labourers make the best soldiers," he said and offered me a bounty of 2½ guineas, which was considerably less that the sixteen we had been expecting so we decided to try the Marines. Their recruiting sergeant promised us 16 guineas bounty when I arrived at their Plymouth headquarters but this did not suit my conductor because, after paying the coach expenses, there would have been nothing left over for him. He asked me what I intended to do, advising me to go back to my master, and forget about the expense he had gone to for me. But I had destroyed the letter so I told him I preferred the 40th Regiment. We went back to the colonel, he gave my companion 2 guineas, and I was sent into barracks.

Next day I received my clothes, and about a week later was sworn in before a magistrate, receiving my bounty at the same time[4]. I was very mistaken about the money lasting.

Shortly afterwards orders came for the regiment to march to Winchester[5]. There we remained for about a month. I had begun to drill twice a day. I soon learnt the foot drill and was then put on musketry drill.

After Winchester, we moved to Portsmouth. We were there a week before being ordered into barracks at Bexhill in Sussex. Our 1st battalion was there[6] and, in order to make it 1000 strong, a number of men were drafted into it from our battalion - the 2nd. I was one of them[7]. Soon orders came for us to go to Portsmouth; we were about to embark on foreign service[8].

- CHAPTER 3 -

In the Light Infantry at Montevideo
October 1806 - February 1807

In 1806, Commodore Sir Home Popham, a commander of the British naval forces and an ambitious adventurer, devised a plan to use Government troops in an expedition against the Spanish in their wealthy South American territories. A small force of 1600 men under Brigadier-General William Carr Beresford sailed in April and, on 27 June, captured Buenos Aires. The British Government, which had not sanctioned the action, now found itself pressured by commercial interests to support and reinforce it with additional troops. This they did, and among those despatched to South America were the men of the 1st battalion of the 40th Regiment.

We spent the night before we sailed in the town. In the morning the bugle sounded for the regiment to assemble and the order to embark was given. Only six women to a company of 100 men were allowed to come with us, so many married men had to leave wives and children behind, with the prospect that they might never see them again. The scenes of parting between husband and wife, father and child, young man and sweetheart, were heart-rending, the last most affected with the least cause. Amid the cheers of the crowd, and with the band playing "The Girl I left behind me," we embarked. As my family did not have the slightest idea where I was, there was no-one to throw so much as a parting glance at me.

Our destination was South America to fight the Spanish. My feelings about going on foreign service for the first time were confused. I was jubilant because I knew my pursuers were outwitted at last, yet I felt timid too, as all young recruits must do in similar circumstances. I wasn't happy at the thought of leaving my country with my family in it, or with the possibility that I might never return.

Next day we drew out of Portsmouth harbour[1]. It wasn't long before many started suffering from sea-sickness and I, worse luck, was one of them. It lasted a whole week. During that time we scarcely ate anything, so when we recovered, our appetites were such that we could have readily finished a donkey with a hamper of greens.

We had good weather until we reached the tropics, when a dead calm followed for a fortnight[2]. As we were nearly upon the Equinoctial line[3], the interesting custom of the shaving ceremony took place. This was no doubt very amusing to those who escaped it by treating the sailors to a bottle of rum, or to those who had crossed the Line before, but to us on whom the barber operated, it was not so pleasant.

A large tub of water was placed on deck and those who were to be shaved sat in turn on the edge. The barber - who was the sailor who had crossed the line most often - stepped forward. He lathered the first face all over with tar and grease, scraped it off with a piece of iron hoop, then pushed the man backwards into the tub. Those so 'shaved' then had to crawl out and sneak off to clean themselves as best they could. It passed off very well because plenty of rum was provided by those officers and men who were more disposed to join in the pay than the play.

During the calms, we amused ourselves fishing for dolphins. We also practised with ball-cartridge for the first time. Our target was a bottle, which was corked and flung overboard. A dollar was offered to the first man to break it. Each man fired once. No-one broke it, but I was the nearest, making the bottle spin round. I got a glass of grog from the major[4] as a reward, but then he asked me what trade I was in before I joined the army. Knowing that I was too far from England to be sent back, I told him the truth; I told him that I was a builder's apprentice.

"So, my boy, you prefer knocking down houses in the enemy's country to putting them up in your own?" he said. At that moment we were having an easy time, but there were many occasions afterwards when I would have liked to have been given the choice of laying bricks again.

After a fortnight of calm weather, a fair wind blew up, and our voyage continued. We had to take on water and provisions so we called at Rio de Janeiro, the capital of the Brazilian Empire[5]. It lay on the western side of the entrance to a fine bay which formed a harbour. While we were anchored there, we went on shore, and the Queen of Portugal reviewed us. Next day, as a present for us, she sent on board onions and pumpkins, which were very welcome.

We were anchored at Rio de Janeiro for about a fortnight before sailing further south to Maldonado where our fleet was to rendezvous. We were joined by 5000 troops under Sir Samuel Auchmuty[6], and the whole fleet moved on to Montevideo.

No time was lost on our arrival. Early the next morning boats were ordered alongside the troopships to convey us to shore[7]. The enemy was waiting on the banks to receive us - at 15,000 strong they were an alarming sight. There seemed nothing but death or glory before us.

The signal was hoisted from the admiral's ship and, under fire from the enemy's artillery, we started for the shore. A few of our men were killed and wounded by the cannon[8], and some of our boats were sunk, but as soon as we struck the shore, we jumped out and formed a line in the water. We fired a volley and charged, driving them from their position on the bank. Spaniards, we discovered, were not that difficult to encounter. Our boats had been ready in case of retreat but,

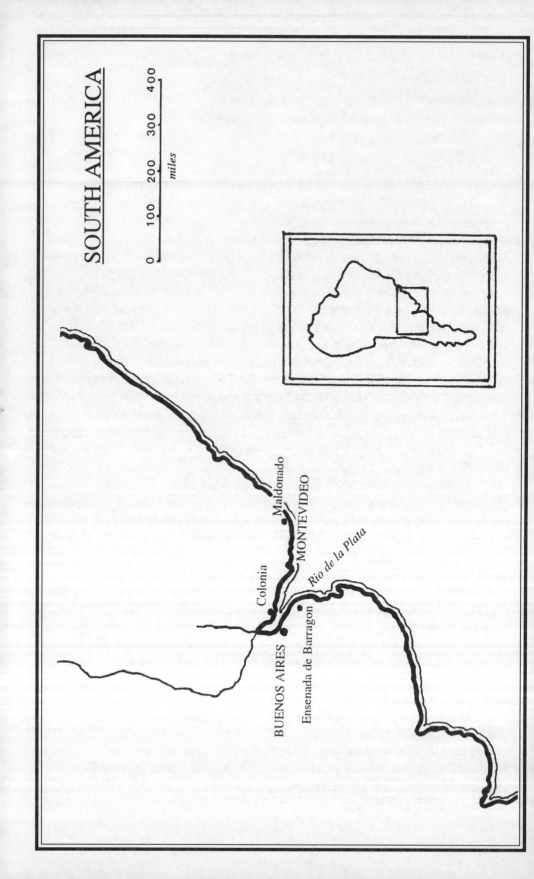

having gained the victory, we had no need of them, and stopped all night on the bank instead.

We had no artillery in that first engagement, but now some field-pieces were sent on shore with a number of sailors with drag-ropes to work them, as we had no horses. The countryside was mostly level and, being green pasture, it was favourable for the sailors who went along pretty easily. This was new work to them and they were in their glory. When the cannon were in place they were fired, making the enemy retreat into the well-fortified town of Montevideo. The body of our army then encamped in a line stretching from sea to sea so that the town - which stood upon a projecting piece of land - was cut off from the mainland[9]. An outlying picket of 300 men was placed in front.

The countryside around us abounded with ducks, geese, turkeys, fowls, sheep and bullocks. As you can imagine, our men found these very providential.

On the third day of our encampment[10], the Spaniards sallied out of the town and made a surprise attack on our picket. Overpowered, our men were obliged to retreat leaving on the field behind them, two wounded grenadiers who, to our horror, the Spaniards deliberately cut to pieces. Our army came up and we charged them. They retreated towards the town, but a terrible slaughter ensued in which we were amply repaid for our two grenadiers. There cannot have been fewer than 3000 Spaniards killed and wounded, for the next day we buried 2000. Our loss was a mere nothing[11].

That night I was a sentry at the road leading to the town, near to a hole in which we had buried 500-600 of the enemy. It was the most uncomfortable two hours' sentry I had spent. Remembering the absurd ghost stories I had heard as a child, I kept a closer watch on the grave than I did on the road. I started to think about things I had done which I should have preferred not to. For the first time, I regretted leaving my apprenticeship and embarking on what I now knew to be such a dangerous life. In getting out of the frying pan, I had found myself in the fire, and I was soon to discover that I had men even more difficult to deal with than my old master. I did become more hardened, but it was at this juncture that I sent my first letter home. I told my family where I was, but kept from them the more perilous parts of my story.

I would like here to warn any master whose eye may fall on this story that by treating a lad who is put under his care too harshly he will discourage him in the occupation he is intended to follow. He will drive him from his home - and perhaps from his country - to his ruin. My master's want of kindness forced me into a very different sort of life to that which my parents intended, and although it wasn't ruinous, it was so perilous that I now look back in wonder that I have been spared to tell my story at all.

After their retreat into the town, the Spaniards never sallied out again, and we set to work building up batteries and breastworks. In order to construct gabions and fascines[12], 300 of us were sent to cut down a nearby copse of peach-trees. It took several days to complete the fortifications then we began bombarding Montevideo with the 24-pounders brought from the man-of-war. After about four days play a breach was made by knocking down the gate and part of the wall, which was six feet thick. The enemy repaired it at night with a quantity of bullocks' hides filled with earth. At 2 o'clock the next morning, we advanced to storm the town[13].

Captain Renny of our regiment[14] commanded the forlorn hope[15], The ladders were placed against the hides of earth - which we preferred to stone - and we scaled them under heavy fire from the Spaniards. Captain Renny was leading the men on when he fell at the breach, but we carried on and succeeded in forcing our way into the town. The streets were soon filled with the reinforcements that followed up[16]. We drove the enemy from the batteries, and massacred with sword or bayonet all whom we found carrying arms - the general's orders had been not to plunder or enter any house, or injure any woman, child, or man not carrying arms. When we reached the gunwharf, we found some twenty or thirty negroes chained to the guns. We spared them and later found them useful for burying the dead.

The worst of the fighting over, the drums beat for the massacre to be stayed and for us to assemble in the square. We were ordered to take prisoner everyone we could lay our hands on. Despatched to the forts and batteries for the purpose, our troops took nearly 3000 prisoners[17].

The governor of the town[18] gave up himself and all his forts, except the citadel, which was commanded by a separate general. To this general Sir Samuel sent a flag of truce asking for his surrender. The answer was "No," so three or four riflemen were placed on a tower nearby with orders to pick him out and shoot him. They spotted the general on the ramparts in full uniform and shot him dead.

Disheartened at losing their commander, the Spaniards lowered the draw-bridge, came out of the citadel, and gave themselves up. Some of our troops immediately took possession, pulling down the Spanish colours and hoisting the English flag in its place[19].

We had taken about 4000 prisoners in all[17]. Among them was an Irishman who had somehow got over to the other side and had been fighting against us. He was tried and sentenced to be hanged. We were marched up to witness his execution and take example from it, but the rope was weak and, when he fell, his weight broke it. As soon as his feet touched ground, he begged for mercy. The rope had made such a terrible mark on his neck that the general decided he had been hanged enough and he was sent into hospital. When he recovered, he was transported for the rest of the life that had been given back to him. While he was on his way down the town to go on board ship, if he had one dollar given him, he had half a peck - not that they were going to be much use to him where he was going. There aren't many men who can say they have been hanged and transported afterwards!

I never heard any more of him. The other prisoners were also sent on board a ship, but I don't know where they were taken[20].

- CHAPTER 4 -

Colonia and San Pedro
February - June 1807

Now that we were in possession of a fine town, we made ourselves at home. All we had to do was put 300-400 men on picket round the walls, and make sure that the gates were closed every night at sunset and not opened again until daylight. The inhabitants were not deprived of their livelihoods - our general issued a proclamation that they should open their shops and carry on their business as usual. If any declined, he kindly sent parties along to do it for them.

We thought Sir Samuel Auchmuty an excellent commander. When told about the barbarity of the Spaniards to our two wounded comrades, he had said we were to repay them in their own coin. Although the fashion at that time was for soldiers to be smart, with long powdered hair, Sir Samuel believed they should be rough-looking, with long beards and greasy haversacks. It was because of his dislike of dandyism that the fashion for powdered hair was done away with soon after we landed in South America. Of course, it might have been that it was difficult to get the powder.

We were in Montevideo for at least five months. During that time, a sergeant and corporal of the Spanish army entered the town in disguise and tried to persuade some of our men to join them. Goodfellow, a sergeant in my regiment, tempted by their heavy bounty, accepted their offer and tried to pass out of the town with them[1]. But they had a most unlucky encounter - they met the general and his staff. The three runaways were in disguise but the general recognised Goodfellow. They were brought back, put under charge, and a court-martial ordered for the next day.

Our colonel begged for the sergeant's life and, on account of the regiment's good conduct in the field, the general granted it, changing his sentence to one of transportation for life. The Spaniards were not so lucky. They were tried and hanged to make sure that they could not repeat their mischievous practices[2].

Another case of desertion was that of an officer's servant who went off, not only with most of his master's clothes, but with a Spanish lady as well. He was luckier; he got away with it. Nothing more was heard of him.

Such temptations were not rare. A Spanish gentleman offered me a fortune - and his daughter - if I would desert and remain in the country. I don't think it mattered to him who his daughter married, as long as someone could be persuaded. He had opportunities to make up to me because I was partially disabled from duty for a fortnight, limping around from a slight wound I had received in the left leg when we stormed the town. When we met, the gentleman treated me to anything I cared to name, and he often gave me money, which was very acceptable. He rode a horse and one day left it tied up near our main guard while he went into a kind of public-house. While he was inside treating some of our men, those who were outside noticed that his stirrups were made of solid gold. Each weighed about a pound. Of course, when the gentleman came out, one was missing. He reported his loss to the colonel and a search was made, but no clue was found. He rode away, as best he could, with only one stirrup. He never did get his daughter married.

After staying in the town for a time, a thousand of us were despatched up the Rio de la Plata[3] to a small place called Colonia, where an army of Spaniards, 4000-5000 strong, was lying. We landed with ease and, after firing a few shots, the enemy retreated leaving the place in our hands, so we again found ourselves in comfortable quarters[4].

We placed 200-300 men round the place as pickets, and fixed a *cheval de frise* - a rather awkward instrument to face if you are not used to it - in the gate[5]. Duty at this place was hard; there were so few of us that those not on picket duty had to build protective batteries.

The picket-house was some distance from the town. It was occupied by a soap-boiler and tallow-chandler who was very good to us. He killed a bullock almost every night and, as he only required the skin and tallow, the rest he gave to us. You can be sure that two hundred hungry men knew what to do with it!

We had passed a quiet week there when, one night, the Spaniards passed our picket secretly in the darkness, fired a volley into the town, and then retreated. Those on picket had just managed to get through safely into the town, but one man had been left asleep in the picket-house. The Spaniards, scouring the place for stragglers, would have killed him if they had found him, but the tallow-chandler concealed him under a quantity of dry hides, and his life was saved[1]. Our reward for being caught out on picket was heavier duty, but our numbers were augmented to help prevent further annoyance.

Two or three days later the tallow-chandler was notified that he would have to join the Spanish army. Before he left, he went to our colonel for advice. The colonel told him he should go but said that if he managed to come back with particulars about the enemy's strength, he would be rewarded. He left, and ten days later was back with the information. I don't know what his reward was but two days later, as a result of his tidings, we were called under arms[7].

It was midnight and each man was given half a pound of beef and ordered to return to his lodgings for two hours, then fall in again. We didn't know where we were going, only that a number of sailors from our ships were to take charge of the town during our absence.

A little after two in the morning we left the town with an Indian guide who we asked, as best we could, where were we going? He gave us to understand that we were on the way to fight some Spaniards, which we had pretty well guessed anyway! He added that we would be encountering about 4000-5000 of them. This was daunting news despite the fact that we had found Spaniards rather cowardly. After marching five or six miles, we despatched skirmishing parties which fell in with the enemy picket, a few of whom were taken prisoner, the rest retreating without doing anything but send up some rockets to warn their main body. We marched on and met their main body at a place called San Pedro. A river separated us, but it wasn't deep and we waded across under the fire of the Spanish cannon, which killed two of our men. Once we were over we formed line and advanced. They stood on some fine rising ground and fired first with their few pieces of cannon and their musketry, but every shot seemed to go over our heads. We were soon up, and at them like dragons, wounding their general and taking about 150 of his men prisoners. We also captured a stand of colours, three pieces of cannon, and their baggage[8]. In their haste, they had left a nice breakfast of fowls, geese, turkeys, beef, rice, and calavancos for us, although the latter - flavoured with cayenne pepper and garlic - were rather too warm for our taste.

The colonel[9] ordered everything to be taken from the prisoners, because that was how he had been served when taken prisoner at Buenos Aires, so we cleared them of all they possessed: their money, which amounted to about 2000 dollars; their clothes; and even their boots.

While the plunder was going on, I entered one of the enemy's store-houses. At one end was a quantity of bullock's hides and between them and the wall was a narrow gap. Beside the hides stood a Spaniard. I knew him well because he had sold cakes to us while we were at Colonia. He now offered me a pot of honey to eat. I had misgivings. Fearing poison, I motioned him to eat first. Meanwhile I cast my eyes to the left. Emerging from between the hides was another Spaniard. He had a pistol and he levelled it at me. I became pretty active, as you can imagine, and guarded the pistol off, but the shot still whizzed very close to my head. I was very angry. The man disappeared back into the hides, but I was determined he should not escape.

At that moment one of our cavalrymen - an Irishman - came in. I told him I had been shot at by a Spaniard hiding behind the hides.

"I'll fetch him out," he said. "You stand at one end ready to stop him with your bayonet."

So Paddy went round with his sword. After a little exercise he sang out, "Look out comrade! He's coming." Sure enough he did and I skewered him to the wall by driving my bayonet right through his body. Paddy came out and finished him by splitting his head nearly in two with his heavy sword.

"Bad luck to ye," said Paddy. "I don't think ye'll ever shoot another Englishman, or Irishman either."

The other man had made off.

Among the things we took were about twenty barrels of gunpowder and a quantity of cigars. These proved a mixed blessing - whilst we were smoking the latter, one of the company wandered too near the former and ignited it with a spark. Twelve men were blown into the air. None were killed, but they were so frightfully burnt that several died on reaching Colonia[10]. I believe the only men killed by the enemy's hand were the two who fell crossing the river[2]. We gave ten dollars to each of the widows of the men who died, and the rest of the prize-money was divided amongst us.

- CHAPTER 5 -

Buenos Aires
June 1807 - June 1808

The number of British troops committed to the campaign in South America was growing all the time. A contingent under the command of General Robert Craufurd, despatched from the Cape of Good Hope on 6 April 1807, was expected to bring the total to over 10,000. As this was Auchmuty's first independent command, the British Government decided that a more senior man should lead them. Much to Auchmuty's surprise, Lt General John Whitelocke arrived in Montevideo on 11 May 1807 to replace him. With him came a further 1800 troops. Whitelocke then awaited the arrival of Craufurd before moving against Buenos Aires with its 40,000 Spanish inhabitants. Buenos Aires was now under the command of French-born Santiago Liniers who recruited an army and built up the city's defences.

With nothing else to be done at San Pedro we returned to Colonia. The three pieces of cannon, laden with our wounded, were dragged back, our prisoners walking along barefoot because we had their boots. When our sailors at Colonia saw how many prisoners there were, and how many cannon we had taken, they saluted us with three cheers. The prisoners were sent on board a ship anchored in the river, and the next day the colonel ordered that everything belonging to them should be brought out, offering a fair price for them to be returned to their proper owners. Apparently, he had only allowed us to take the things as an example.

We remained comfortably in the town until General Whitelocke came out from England with a reinforcement[1]. He took command from Sir Samuel Auchmuty and, leaving some troops in charge of Montevideo, ordered the rest of our army2 to Buenos Aires. It stopped at Colonia on the way to pick up our little squad.

We landed some miles away from Buenos Aires[3] with the intention of storming the back of the town, as the side that faced the coast was strongly fortified. We marched inland and set up our first encampment not far from where we landed[4].

While we were here, a corporal and two privates were in the act of plundering one of the Indian huts when they were set upon by the inhabitants, who were armed. The corporal was lassoed around the neck and dragged away, one private was knocked down and stabbed, and the other was wounded by a sabre which took the skin and hair off the back of his head. He escaped and got back to the regiment, but the natives started using the corporal's gun and ammunition to fire into our camp. Fortunately for us, it was a harmless practice.

We resumed our march the next day and encamped that night, which happened to be very foggy. A party went out in search of bullocks for the army. In the darkness an Indian lassoed the mounted officer with them. The officer had the presence of mind to ride after the Indian so that he could not be pulled over, and he managed to cut the lasso with his sword.

Next day, we were followed on our march by about 200 Indians, the foremost of which not only wore our corporal's jacket, but carried his head on a pole. I don't know why. Perhaps the Indians thought more of a dead man's head than we feel disposed to?

We carried on, through a great many orange-gardens, till we came to a lane thickly hedged on both sides, which we entered by a gate. It was a good place to ambush the Indians so, after the body of our army had passed through, a few men - myself included - waited for them. A reserve was placed a short distance away in case of combat. There were less than twenty of us so I rather shook in my shoes when I saw how many Indians were approaching. We did not understand what they said but we could see they had misgivings. Directly the front party had passed the gate, we fired. We killed two of them and wounded their chief, the man who was so proud of the corporal's head; the rest fled for their lives. We picked up the wounded man and later left him, more dead than alive, in a neighbouring village.

On nearing Buenos Aires the Light Brigade, under the command of Colonel Pack, was ordered on in front. I was with the main body of the army and did not enter the city myself so I could not see what was going on, but we heard the muskets and fell under arms waiting for the general's orders to advance[5].

Buenos Aires was only lightly fortified towards the country and therefore was easier to take than Montevideo. Apparently, the Light Brigade succeeded in taking the Bull Ring battery. There had been some cannons placed at the end of each street, but they were overcome. After passing these, our soldiers took possession of the city and hoisted the King's flag on a convent. Then they waited, expecting the body of our army to come up. But it didn't. Instead of following up and relieving the brigade as he should have done, General Whitelocke camped a mile out of the town and remained there. We lay there all night, not doing a stroke. The Spaniards, meanwhile, rallied and overpowered the Brigade[6].

Next day we re-embarked for Montevideo, ignorant of the fact that terms had been agreed with the Spanish[7].

We remained at Montevideo for two months. The ships taken in the harbour were offered for sale but as the inhabitants refused to buy them, we loaded them with hides, tallow, and cocoa (and anything else not worth bringing home), towed them out to the mouth of the harbour, and set fire to them. Previously the Spaniards had blown up a very fine frigate to prevent it falling into our hands. Part of our army

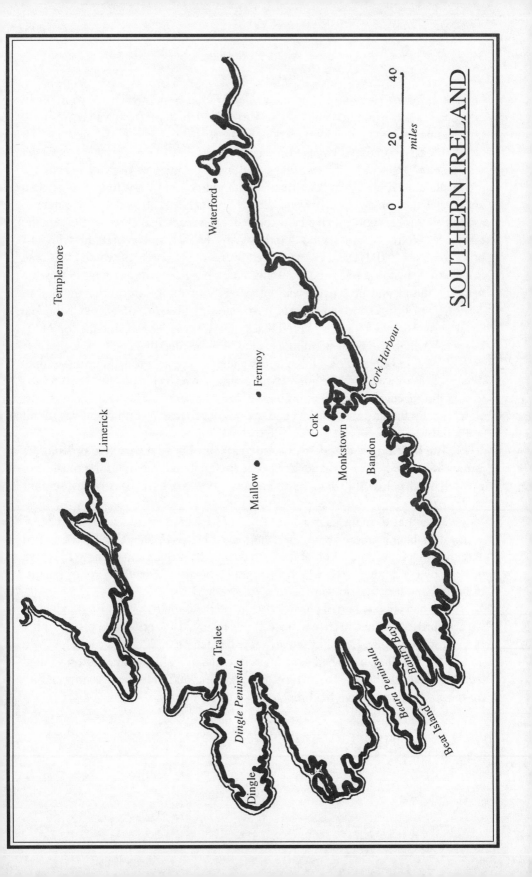

SOUTHERN IRELAND

embarked for the East Indies and the Cape of Good Hope, whilst we went on an expedition about a hundred miles up the Rio de la Plata to get fresh water. When we returned we started on our journey homewards[8].

The first part of our voyage was very pleasant and, in general, the troops kept very healthy. However, when we had sailed some distance, we had a dead calm for a considerable time. As a consequence our journey not only took longer than anticipated but our water ran low and had to be rationed to half a pint a day. Luckily, a small additional supply arrived unexpectedly. The captain had seen a cloud in the distance. "We're going to have a thunderstorm," he said, and ordered the scupper-holes to be stopped. He sent everyone below except the watch, of which I was one. Soon, it began to thunder and lightning and the rain fell in torrents. It was the heaviest thunderstorm I had ever witnessed. Lightning struck the mainmast, splitting a piece off from top to bottom, and striking dead one of our men while he sat at mess. His mess tin was burned black, his shirt was singed, and the top of his bayonet - which had been standing close to him - melted like lead[9].

The rain lasted two or three hours and we were able to bale up more than twenty casks of water, whose quality was not improved by the fact that pigs, fowls, geese, and turkeys had been roaming the decks. In our parched state it was still welcome, for up until then we had had to cook our food and wash ourselves in salt water only.

The lightning had shaken our little bark terribly so the captain ordered the pumps to be tried. There was no leakage to be found, but the lightning must have got well down below, for when the main hatchway was opened, the smell of sulphur was suffocating.

After the storm the calm continued, and we had to amuse ourselves fishing. A few days later a breeze sprang up, but it was foul for England, and we knocked about waiting for a more favourable one. It eventually arrived and got us to the Cove of Cork by Christmas 1807, which we spent on board. We sent ashore for raisins, flour, fat, and beer and so were able to enjoy ourselves.

We had already laid in our sea stock in preparation to start for England when we were ordered to land in Ireland instead. We marched to Cork and to various other places for six months[10], nothing of any note happening until orders came for us to go to Portugal. Bonaparte had overrun Portugal and Spain, and the nation we had recently been fighting in Montevideo, Buenos Aires and Colonia, was now calling for our assistance to drive the French out of their country.

- CHAPTER 6 -

Vimeiro, and into the Grenadier Company
July 1808 - April 1809

Napoleon Bonaparte 1769-1821, a former artillery officer in the French Army and later General of the Republican Armies, had crowned himself Emperor of France in 1804. As well as having dependent territories, he sought to influence policy in neighbouring countries, demanding in 1807 that the Portuguese break off relations with Britain and impose a prohibition on British goods. When the Portuguese refused, he declared war on them (20 October 1807), and in November, a French army of 30,000 men under General Soult marched through Spain - then an ally of France - into Portugal. The Portuguese royal family, and a large number of senior army officers, fled to Brazil. By December, the French were occupying Lisbon.

Napoleon, no longer content to have Spain as an ally, decided to rule it instead. In March 1808 he sent 100,000 troops over the border and forced the King of Spain to abdicate, appointing his brother Joseph Bonaparte in his place. The Spanish people were outraged, but their rebellions were ruthlessly put down by French soldiers. Spanish provincial governments, called 'juntas', appealed for assistance, and in June 1808 sent a deputation to Britain. A Portuguese deputation, on the same errand, followed in July. They pleaded for joint action against the French invaders. Britain agreed and Sir Arthur Wellesley, who had assembled a British force at Cork ready to sail to South America to fight against Spanish interests, was ordered to redirect his forces to Portugal to protect them instead.

We embarked at Cork Harbour and waited for the English fleet to gather. About 12,000 strong[1], we sailed on 12 July 1808 under the command of Sir Arthur Wellesley

We touched at Corunna[2] to make arrangements with the Spaniards. Their advice was to land in Portugal, so we went to Mondego Bay and landed near the town of Figueira[3], leaving our baggage on board. After a five day march, we were joined by General Spencer[4]. Next day our advanced guard had a slight engagement with the enemy at Roliça[5]. We marched on to Vimeiro, and were joined by Generals Anstruther and Acland with more reinforcements. Sir Hugh Dalrymple took command from Sir Arthur Wellesley.

The village of Vimeiro stood in a valley with a fine range of hills to the west, and a ridge of heights to the east. Our brigades were stationed on the mountains to the west, our cavalry were posted in the valley, and General Anstruther's brigade lay to the east.

On the first night of our encampment, I was strolling over the hills with two comrades when we found a hive of bees. We carried it back into camp, but not without difficulty, for it must have weighed at least a hundred-weight, and the bees were very uncivil passengers[6]. Our faces and hands were fearfully stung, but our honey and grapes - for we also profited from being camped in some fine vineyards - were some compensation. Next morning we started to breakfast off our finds but were disturbed by the approach of the enemy, and ordered under arms[7].

The right of our line was involved in fighting at least two hours before the engagement became general and included us on the left side, but all that time, we were skirmishing with the enemy[8]. I remember it well because a Frenchman and myself were firing at each other for at least half an hour without injury. He once took a pretty straight aim at me, and had the bullet not embedded itself in the trunk of a cork-tree, behind which I was standing, it would have proved fatal.

"Well done, front-rank man," I said to the tree, "thee doesn't fall at that stroke."

Soon afterwards, a comrade came up and asked how I was getting on.

"Badly," I said and told him that there was a Frenchman in front, and that we had been trying to knock each other over for some time. He asked me to let him try so I pointed out the thicket he was hiding behind. Unfortunately for the Frenchman, my comrade was left-handed. Making sure that he too was covered by my old front-rank man, he put his rifle to his left shoulder. By-and-by Mr Frenchman again made his peep round the bush. It was his last. My comrade killed him with the first shot.

We had been skirmishing for some time when a large body of French made their appearance in our front. Our artillery greeted them pretty sharply by ploughing furrows through them with ball, which threw them into a confused state. Our column, under General Spencer, then advanced with our cannon still playing over our heads. When we got within a short distance, we fired and charged them. The fighting was severe and kept up for some time, but we drove them from the position they occupied, capturing about seven pieces of cannon, and some ammunition waggons. The French loss cannot have been less than two thousand, but it is very hard to arrive at a just calculation. Our loss was reported to have been about 700[9].

When the battle was over we marched to Lisbon, passing about 150 carts laden with the enemy's wounded. When we arrived we encamped. The French had no means of communicating with the city because our fleet was lying in or near the mouth of the harbour, and our army was stopping all approaches from the land. The French in the city were blocked in. On our first night the inhabitants illuminated the part where we lay.

We were not destined to be outside the city long because the leaders of the armies came to some terms and, in September, the French - the very troops with whom we later had to contend - embarked at the harbour with the honours of war[10]. When they quit Lisbon, we took up quarters in the city[11], amid the joy of the inhabitants. They shouted in triumph as the French left, and for several nights afterwards held illuminations on the vessels in the harbour.

Lisbon was situated on the right bank of the Tagus, near the mouth, which forms a very fine harbour. It stood chiefly on precipitous hills, the highest of which was occupied by the fine castle of St George, which attracted the eye from everywhere in the city. The great squares contained some magnificent edifices, with very fine pillars. The streets were narrow and winding and dirty. At that time the city still exhibited marks of the terrible earthquake which almost destroyed it in 1755 and, although the French had left it in a desolate state, the general view from the harbour was very beautiful. The buildings extended for nearly two miles along the coast, and the sides of the hills were clothed with plantations and numberless vineyards.

Sir Hugh Dalrymple, Sir Arthur Wellesley, and some of the other leaders of our army were soon recalled to England to explain the terms of the agreement arrived at in Portugal[12] because people in England had received the first reports with indignation. An inquiry was held and Sir Arthur Wellesley was chosen as the best person to take the command of the troops in the Peninsula.

During our stay in Lisbon our regiment fell ill and was unfit for service for about two months[13]. During that time, Sir John Moore's army had been repulsed by sheer force of numbers and he himself killed at Corunna[14]. We, and 5000 Spaniards, were ordered into Spain. We had a long and tedious march to a place called Seville where we encamped for several weeks[15].

In Seville, without leave to, I absented myself from guard for 24 hours and landed myself in a fine scrape. When I returned I was put into the guard-room, and a drum-head court-martial was ordered on me. It was my first offence but that did not screen me - my sentence was 400 lashes.

On hearing this I felt ten times worse than I ever did on entering a battle-field. My life seemed of very little consequence and I thought of my home and my days as an apprentice. Had I been sentenced to be shot, I would not have despaired more. The guards brought me to the square of the convent where my sentence was to be carried out and where the regiment was already assembled to witness my punishment. The judgement was read over me by the colonel and I was ordered to strip. Hardened by that time, I did so without the help that was offered and was lashed to the halberds. The colonel gave the order for the drummers to commence. Each drummer gave me 25 lashes in turn. I bore it well but, by the time I had received 175, I became so enraged with pain that I pushed the halberds. They were only planted on stones and did not stand firm so I moved them right across the square amid the laughter of the regiment.

The colonel[16], judging that I had had sufficient, ordered "the sulky rascal down." Indeed I was sulky for, although the blood ran down my trousers, I had not given vent to a single sound. I was unbound and the corporal hove my shirt and jacket over my shoulders, then conveyed me - a miserable spectacle - to the hospital.

Perhaps the flogging was a good thing in preventing me from committing greater crimes, which might have earned me even more severe punishments. Nevertheless, it was a great trial for me. A lot of that kind of punishment could have been abandoned by the army. It is hard to believe that 400 lashes could be ordered on a man as young as I[17], one who had undergone all the privations of a most bloody war, for a first offence, which could have been overlooked or dealt with by a severe reprimand[18].

I was in hospital for about three weeks. When I came out - still in a very marked state, of which I bear the remembrances on my back to this day - I was transferred from the Light into the Grenadier company[19].

- CHAPTER 7 -

A Grenadier at Talavera, and an Invalid at Elvas
April - November 1809

After Sir John Moore's defeat in northern Spain in January, the French invaded Portugal again, capturing Oporto in the north. Sir Arthur Wellesley, now commander of the British forces on the Iberian Peninsula, returned to Portugal on 22 April 1809 and marched his army north to liberate Oporto from Marshal Soult. He succeeded, and forced the French to retreat back into Spain. Marshal Victor's army was in the Talavera region of Spain. Wellesley, and his Spanish ally General Gregorio Garcia de la Cuesta, decided to combine and go after it. The 40th Regiment were recalled from Seville to join them.

When we left Seville[1], we marched to Cadiz and encamped. That night an English wine-merchant asked the officers to dine with him[2]. He also offered each man in our regiment a pint of wine, and each woman half that quantity, plus a pound of bread apiece, so we were drawn up in line and marched into a tremendous cellar. There were two doors, one at each end. We entered at one, received our share, and went out by the other. After drinking to the merchant's little kindness, we slept soundly.

Next day we embarked at Cadiz. When we landed at Lisbon we went some miles up the country to join Sir Arthur's army in Castelo Branco.

The 40th left Lisbon on 15 June, were transported up the river to Santarem, then continued on foot to Abrantes where they encamped. Wellesley's army started its march into Spain on 27 June, crossing the border on 4 July, to combine with Cuesta at Oropesa, 10 miles from Talavera, on 21 July. Between them they had 55,000 men.

Totalling about 20,000 English and about 60,000 Allies we advanced across a fine plain, each band playing before its own regiment. Sir Arthur Wellesley took the opportunity to review the Spanish troops as they passed. They looked fine enough but, as we knew from Montevideo and Colonia, they were fit for nothing but falling into disorder and confusion, either because they weren't properly disciplined, or because their officers were no good.

The plain we crossed must have been famous for hares for it swarmed with them. They ran in all directions, even into our lines. They are stupid animals when frightened as they were then by the noise our men made. I killed one with the muzzle of my musket and sold it to my captain for a dollar.

We often saw signs of where the enemy had camped, and encamped at or near the same places ourselves. They were usually close to some river, or other large supply of water, a small supply being of little use to such a large body of men and horses. However, we never actually caught sight of the French until we got to Talavera where, on the 27th and 28th of July 1809, we engaged them.

At the Battle of Talavera, our line extended for about two miles and, at times, all of it was to be involved. It was especially hot for us because many Spaniards threw down their arms and fled[3].

We camped on the ground we occupied, but that night the French made an unexpected attack on us and nearly gained the heights. We repulsed them but, expecting another attack any minute, had to lie on our arms.

Very early next morning, an altercation occurred between the French and Spaniards but it did not last long. A little later, at about 5 or 6 o'clock, the French columns were seen in motion on our left. They ascended the height to attack us but were driven back by the heavy fire of our muskets, leaving the ground strewn with their dead. At 11 or 12 o'clock the firing ceased and a truce allowed both armies to collect their wounded and convey them to the rear. There, inter-mixed, a friendly intercourse sprang up between them, the Allies and French even shaking hands with one another.

At 1 or 2 o'clock the battle recommenced with a heavy cannonade and an attack on the whole British line. After some very brisk fighting, we repulsed them for the third time and they had to retreat with a loss of thousands, and a few pieces of cannon. The British loss was about a 1000 killed and 3000-4000 wounded[4]. After the battle, something dreadful occurred: the long dry grass in which the wounded were lying caught fire and many who should have been conveyed to hospital in Talavera, were scorched to death.

That night we expected to see our noble enemy again, but we were mistaken. They took off and, in the morning, only their rear-guard was to be seen. The Spanish general, Cuesta, ordered the battalions who had fled to be decimated but, after an entreaty by Sir Arthur Wellesley, only about 40 were killed. Cuesta needed quite as much leading as his men; he could be obstinate and would refuse to fight when called upon to do so by Sir Arthur[5].

The French army of Marshal Victor had been defeated at Talavera, but the allies were not strong enough to pursue it. Moreover, King Joseph Bonaparte's army was on the move, and that of Marshal Soult had been reformed, re-equipped, and was now threatening the Allied army's supply line from Portugal. Wellesley felt that Soult's army was the greatest threat and decided to confront it, but circumstances turned what began as a positive march out of Spain into a steady withdrawal.

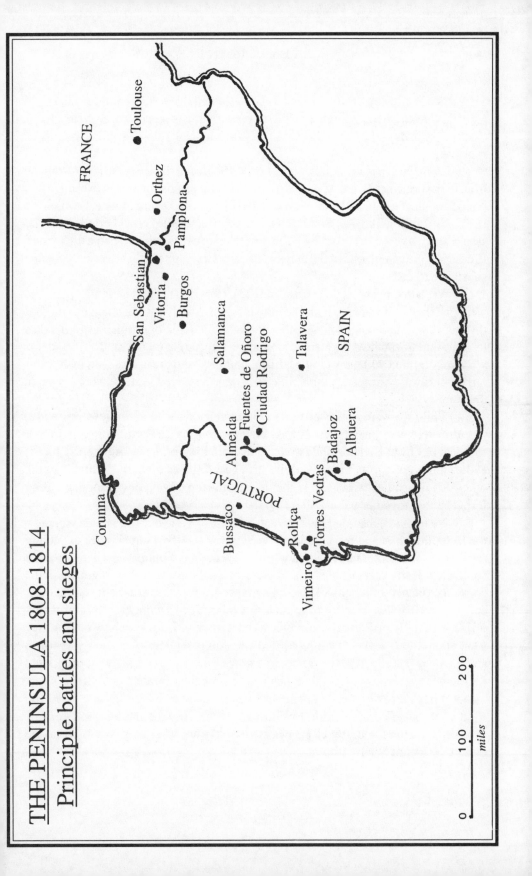

THE PENINSULA 1808-1814
Principle battles and sieges

FRANCE

● Toulouse

● Orthez

● Pamplona

San Sebastian ●
Vitoria ●
● Burgos

● Salamanca

● Fuentes de Oñoro
● Ciudad Rodrigo

● Talavera

SPAIN

● Almeida

● Badajoz
● Albuera

PORTUGAL

Corunna

● Bussaco
● Roliça
● Torres Vedras
Vimeiro ●

0   100   200

miles

Sir Arthur Wellesley decided to leave Talavera and the wounded in the charge of General Cuesta and on 3 August we set off for Oropesa, where he expected to engage Soult. Within days, he heard that Cuesta had abandoned Talavera, unnecessarily as it proved[6].

From Oropesa, the country was very difficult and the army suffered from the heat, exposure, insufficient food and bad roads[7]. Our provisions rarely exceeded two pounds of meat a day, and was often a pound of meat and a pint of wheat, which we cooked by boiling like rice. Sometimes, we would crack the kernel between two flat stones and make a thick paste by boiling it. On rare occasions, we had a little flour. Illness was prevalent; one of the major causes was having so little bread or vegetable substance to eat[8].

We halted near Val de la Casa and then, two days later, at Deleitosa, then we were marched to Xaracego. It had been so long since we had had a change of clothes that ours were threadbare and smothered in vermin. Lack of provisions obliged us to go to Badajoz, where we arrived after about a fortnight on the road[9]. At Badajoz we were supplied with new clothes, linen, blankets, and great-coats, and when our old clothes were burned, as much livestock was destroyed as there were troops in the country!

While we were at Badajoz, many of us fell sick with a kind of fever and I, unfortunately, was one of them. I was conveyed to Elvas, a Portuguese town about four leagues from Badajoz and two leagues from the frontier with Spain. Situated at the summit of a lofty hill, it was the strongest fortified town in Portugal. At the other side of a valley was a still higher hill, on the top of which was another strong fort. The two together were called Elvas.

We invalids occupied the convents of the town and our loss, made worse by the lack of doctors and medicine, was very great[10]. After about six weeks, having recovered sufficiently to get about a little, I went on the ramparts. There a fearful spectacle met my gaze: the dead - completely naked - were being brought out of the convents, pitched into carts like so many pieces of wood, carried out of the town, and interred in holes scarcely large enough to admit such a number. This unpleasant office fell chiefly on Portuguese convicts and it surprised me to see how readily they went about their work, carrying one body at a time, the legs over their shoulders, and the head dangling down behind. The grave - the piece of ground appropriated for the burials - was so small that they had to pack their burdens with the greatest nicety. I had narrowly escaped being handled in this way by these same men. The sight was quite a cure; I couldn't wait to get back to my regiment at Badajoz![11]

It was after the Battle of Talavera that Sir Arthur Wellesley was raised to the rank of Viscount Wellington[12].

- CHAPTER 8 -

Bussaco, and 'Tom'
November 1809 - September 1810

At the beginning of 1810 we went from Badajoz to Olivenza where we were billeted on the inhabitants, two or more to a house[1]. At the time the names of the drum-majors of the three regiments were Sun, Moon, and Star. Our regiment had the Moon[2], the 53rd the Sun, and the 9th the Star. If having the Sun, Moon, and Star fighting on our side was of any help, then they were there already!

I was billeted with a Welsh comrade called Lewis Phillips[3], in a house occupied by a poor but respectable man and his wife who, on the whole, were very kind to us. They were labourers and, at that season, were employed picking olive-berries. Before going out to work every morning they prepared their supper. It was Lent and, as it was against their religion to eat meat at that time, their supper consisted of greens, oil, cayenne pepper, and salt. This they left on the embers in an earthenware jar so that it would be cooked by the time they came back. If either myself or Phillips were around, they would ask us to give it an occasional stir.

One day, I was the 'cook' and feeling mischievous I took some of my meat - not much because a pound was all we received - cut it up very small, and put it in the jar. By night-time it was so boiled and stirred that even I could scarcely recognize it. When the man and his wife returned they were very hungry and partook of the *caldo*, as they called it. When they pronounced it to be very good, I told them there was meat in it. If I had known what a bother I would create I would never have spoken. They exclaimed that they had eaten the Devil (having been in the country so long, we were beginning to understand their language pretty well), got rid of all they had eaten, and reported me to their priest. He came to the house, condemned me as an ignorant Protestant and told them not to worry, as they had eaten the meat against their will. They never liked me much after that. Unable to get rid of me they still managed to make me feel uncomfortable, although they never set me to watch their *caldo* again. But that did not stop my jokes - I decided it was Lewis' turn.

Lewis and I were seldom on duty together, so it used to fall to the one off duty to do the cooking for the one who was on. One day when I was the cook, I pitched upon a plan to take Mr Taffy in. I asked him what he wanted for his dinner. He said potatoes fried in butter, a piece of bread, and his usual pint of wine. I liked olive oil and Lewis did not, but I fried the potatoes in it anyway. I took him the meal during his break from sentry duty; he was very hungry so wasn't long lapping it up.

"Did you enjoy that, Lewis?" I asked him.

"I've never had a better meal in my life," he replied.

"But I thought you didn't like oil?"

"No more I do!" he replied. "There was no oil in there!"

I told him I had fried the potatoes in it. He wouldn't believe me so I said that, if he was agreeable, I would make another mess in the same manner. When the opportunity arose, I started my frying and he witnessed it. After that he could eat as much oil as I could so my experiment with Lewis succeeded better than that with the worthy people of the house.

Our stay at Olivenza - chiefly to refresh ourselves after our illnesses, the fighting, and the long and tedious marches - lasted a few weeks, then Lord Wellington moved his headquarters to Viseu while most of the army went into cantonments in the valley of the Mondego.

With the troops only strong enough for defensive operations, and being without reinforcements, Lord Wellington made no rash moves and when the enemy invaded Portugal again, he shifted his headquarters to Celorico. From there we moved on to another small place called Guarda, which was near Almeida, about eight or ten leagues from Ciudad Rodrigo[4].

Almeida was garrisoned by Portuguese troops commanded by an English officer. Although the French invested it, Lord Wellington expected it to retard the enemy until the commencement of the rainy season. Massena opened fire on it about 23 August. It was a town of very great strength but was obliged to capitulate on the 27 August when a magazine containing most of the ammunition blew up, taking with it a great part of the town and the fortifications[7].

As Ciudad Rodrigo had also fallen into the enemy's hands[8], Lord Wellington's plan was disappointed and we had to fall back into the valley of the Mondego. Heavy rains and bad roads made it a difficult march but he took us by the best road whereas Massena, who was following us up, took the very worst. We crossed the Mondego River and, about the middle of September, took up a position on the heights of Bussaco, about six leagues north-east of Coimbra. By the 26 September our line was formed. Massena, ignorant of the country, was not expecting to meet either a range of heights, or us on the top of them ready to retard his progress.

Our Division - the 4th - under General Cole[9], occupied the extreme left of the Bussaco heights; we overlooked flat country where the British cavalry were drawn up in reserve. The divisions of Generals Hill, Leith, and Picton occupied the right of our line. The 1st Division - commanded by Sir Brent Spencer - was in the centre. The French had taken up a position in front and we had a splendid view of their encampment. Early on the morning of the 27 October they were astir so we were ordered under arms.

The action commenced on our right and centre, and that was where the heaviest fire was throughout the entire battle, our division having only slight brushes with the enemy. That night, disheartened by their lack of success, the French - who must have lost 4000-5000 men - retreated to their old position. We lost little more than a thousand, but those heights were an immense advantage for we could witness their every movement. The next day they seemed disinclined to renew the contest. There were a few slight engagements, but they were chiefly on the left where the light infantry were.

It was while strolling about on these heights that I caught a fine cock. I tamed him by tying him to my knapsack by the leg, which amused my comrades very much. After a fortnight he would sit there quietly without the string. We named him Tom and I took to carrying him about everywhere, even on to the battlefield. Wherever my knapsack went, Tom went too, but he did not like it when the balls whizzed about. Then he would make the curious noise such birds make when they are pursued or frightened.

His peculiar little ways whiled away many a dreary hour, and we all became very fond of him. He grew quite fat on the many tit-bits he received from us and we marvelled at how he went to each of us in turn for a contribution. More curious still was how he was always ready for action when he saw the knapsacks on the move. He seldom made a mistake about which was mine, but then, after inhabiting it for some time, he had made sufficient marks on it to ensure that *I* could never mistake it either!

CHAPTER 9

Torres Vedras, and the Plunder at Patamara
September 1810 - March 1811

Bussaco was a victory for the Allies whose casualties were 1250 to the 4600 suffered by the French, but Massena's army was still large enough to make a retreat further into Portugal prudent. Wellington had anticipated and prepared for it. Defensive earthworks in the Torres Vedras region north of Lisbon - already a formidable landscape - had been ordered, and 10,000 Portuguese peasants had been at work building them. It was to these Lines, where he knew his men could be well supplied from Lisbon, that Wellington directed his army, drawing Massena's army after him across a countryside denuded of everything that might be of use to them.

From Bussaco Lord Wellington started to retreat towards Lisbon[1]. With the area about to fall within the bounds of the enemy's march, he issued a proclamation ordering the inhabitants to destroy anything of use to the French and to fall back with us. Thousands fled from their dwellings and our army was accompanied by crowds of miserable men, women, and children who were fearful that, if they fell into the hands of the French, they would be treated as others had before - with all the barbarity of an atrocious enemy.

I have heard of moving, and in England have seen carts or wagons loaded with furniture, being driven by a man at about three miles an hour, with a woman and perhaps several children sitting on top or at the back, but never before or since have I seen such a wholesale move as I witnessed then. Everyone was anxious to carry as many of their effects as they could find room for and the farther we went, the more confused our retreat appeared. So exhausted were the multitudes that some had to rest by the roadside, when only the sound of the enemy's approach made them again eager to renew their tedious journey. Some were found dying, or dead, from their exertions. The road everywhere was strewn with the furniture which the poor fugitives had vainly attempted to get forward.

We passed Coimbra - where the French later left thousands of their sick and wounded in hospital, only to have them captured by the Portuguese - and continued south, again crossing the Mondego[2].

We also passed a nunnery, where we halted for about a quarter of an hour. With the French following us up so closely, skirmishing with our rear guard which consisted mostly of cavalry, the colonel ordered the doors to be broken open by a body of grenadiers, of which I was one. The nuns were watching from balconies so crowded that there was an accident and one fell. The poor women seemed glad of their liberty and came out as thick as a flock of sheep. Fearful of the consequences if they took any other direction, many passed us on their way to Lisbon.

We reached Leiria on 2 October. From there it was a long and tedious - but impressive - march to Torres Vedras where we took up our position at some fine breastworks which had been thrown up by the Portuguese peasantry on the orders of Lord Wellington, in case of our retreat[3]. How we needed them! On 10 October, the French came in sight. We were determined that they should proceed not one step farther towards Lisbon. Massena thought he was going to drive the English into the sea, so he was surprised by our strength. He encamped about a mile and a half from our position but, on 14 October, he attacked our lines near Sobral. He was repulsed. A slight skirmish took place on the right of the line and the French general, St Croix, was killed by fire from our gunboats, but our position was so strong that the French chose not to come to a general engagement.

The cold and rainy weather set in but Lord Wellington had provided for us as well as he could; we were so near Lisbon that we had supplies in abundance. We were mostly in cantonments, whilst the men in Massena's army were subject to hardships of the worst description. It was cold and wet, and they had insufficient food and raiment - they were far away from their own country, and the guerillas and mountain rebels were always on the look-out, ready to intercept any supplies sent to them[4].

Our regiment was situated in the front of our works in a village called Patamara where, despite being so near the enemy, we were as comfortable as if we were living in peaceful times. We often wandered into the same vineyards as them and exchanged compliments by shaking hands.[5]

We were cantoned in a large cellar. Unfortunately it was empty, or at least it had no wine in it. There was a vat with a quantity of wheat but as we had plenty of our own supplies we had no need of it.

The owner of our cellar visited us every day and we could not help noticing that he paid particular attention to a large box or bin that two of our men were sleeping in. One morning, we moved it. As the ground underneath had been disturbed, we thought some treasure must be concealed there, so we went to work with our bayonets. We soon came across a large jar containing bags of dollars - about 250 in each bag - We shared them out amongst ourselves, then broke the jar, reburied it in the same place, and put the chest back on the top of it. No-one would have known it had been disturbed.

Next morning, as usual, the owner arrived. He had two labourers with him and these he set to work filling the chest with wheat from the vat to make it weighty, little suspecting that his treasure was no longer underneath but had been divided amongst his tenants. We thought we were free from detection but the restless owner must have dreamt of our manoeuvre for the next morning he appeared again and got the two labourers to shift the wheat back into the vat. They moved the chest, raised the earth, and he found the broken jar.

The man fell into such a terrible rage that he actually tore out some of his hair by the roots, which he must have found a poor way of showing his spite.

"Ladrone! Ladrone!" he cried, which meant Thief! Thief!

We took no notice of him, so he went to report his loss to the colonel. At least he tried to - the colonel did not understand Portuguese. By that time I was well acquainted with the language so he sent for me and asked what the man wanted. I said he wanted a corporal and three privates to guard a stack of wood. The colonel told me to tell him it was nothing to do with him. I told the Portuguese that it was no use him making a noise about the money, which probably hadn't been much, because he had no witnesses to prove he had put it in the cellar in the first place, but he was only appeased for the night and, next morning, went bothering the colonel again. I was sent for.

"What on earth does this man want now!" the colonel asked me.

I was obliged to tell him, but I first asked the colonel if he would forgive me for not having been more truthful. He consented, so I told him the Portuguese said he had lost a lot of money - about 7000 dollars. The Portuguese said he had put the money in the cellar, but as he could bring no witnesses to prove it, the colonel said he could not help.

The man went away but was back again the next morning. To keep him quiet, the colonel told him that the grenadiers were receiving some prize money in a few days, and he could have that in lieu of what he had lost. That satisfied the old man and he shook hands all round, bowing and scraping as if we were kings.

The matter did not rest there. The colonel now suspected we were implicated and next day ordered us out as if we were about to leave. We knew it was a trick because the French were still at our front, so we concealed our shares of the money in and around the cellar. There was a heap of pumpkins in the cellar and myself and a fellow-comrade cut out of one of them a piece large enough to admit the dollars, closed it up with the top of the original piece, then mixed it with the remainder. The company was marched out into a field. Our knapsacks and pockets were searched, but nothing was found, not even the little money some must have had before!

We had baffled them. The colonel did not mind, but the major did and he told the colonel that he would find the money. He was cunning, but the men were artful and, as everyone in the cellar company had taken part in the affair, it was in the interests of all to keep it secret.

The major approached one of the sergeants and told him to pick out the ten men most likely to inform. The sergeant chose the ten worst rogues in the company and marched them off to the major's quarters where they were seen one by one. The

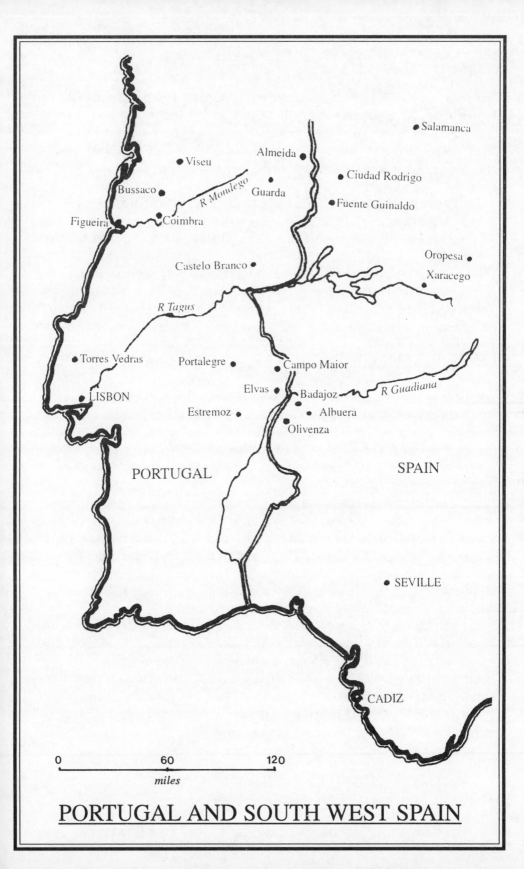

Salamanca

Almeida

Viseu

Ciudad Rodrigo

Bussaco

Guarda

Fuente Guinaldo

Figueira

Coimbra

R Mondego

Oropesa

Castelo Branco

Xaracego

R Tagus

Torres Vedras

Portalegre

Campo Maior

R Guadiana

Elvas

Badajoz

LISBON

Estremoz

Albuera

Olivenza

PORTUGAL

SPAIN

SEVILLE

CADIZ

0   60   120
miles

PORTUGAL AND SOUTH WEST SPAIN

major sat at his table, on which was lying five guineas. This he offered to the first man who would reveal the mystery, but their shares in the cellar prize were worth more. He interviewed about three of them but they all told the same tale, that they knew nothing about the money. Enraged, he called them a set of thieves. Much to the amusement of both the colonel and the regiment, he had to admit he had been beaten in his undertaking[6].

For over a month, Massena remained in his position in front of Torres Vedras, unable to get supplies through Spain because of the guerillas, a most warlike and independent race of Spaniards. Comprised largely of offenders who had escaped to the mountains, they had formed themselves into a body thousands strong and were always on the look out for supplies - particularly those of the enemy - which they then appropriated for their own use. Credit is due to Lord Wellington for drawing the enemy to a place like Torres Vedras, where neither supplies nor advantage could be gained, but where instead they would lose thousands out of want, and exposure to the cold and wet.

In November 1810, Massena was obliged to retrace his steps and withdrew his army to Santarem on the Tagus, about ten leagues from Torres Vedras[7]. He sent out foraging parties to scour the country but his army was so large that this method of gathering provisions was soon exhausted. They committed horrible excesses on the inhabitants, carrying away not only their cattle, but any provisions they could lay their hands on. The infuriated inhabitants retaliated by butchering, or using in a most awful manner, any French stragglers or wounded French soldiers they came across[8].

Leaving some troops in charge of his lines at Torres Vedras, Lord Wellington followed Massena to Santarem. Several small engagements took place but the enemy seemed secure so Lord Wellington moved his army into cantonments for the winter. Our detachment was on the Tagus, some distance from Santarem[9]. While we were there we received our South American prize money. Each private received eight dollars and I believe the sergeants had sixteen. The money, taken from those who were now our allies, was now spent amongst them[10].

The Lisbon traders got scent of this and a quantity of boats, laden with little requisites and luxuries, came down the river so we soon managed to rid ourselves of our little spare cash. Our colonel, determined to prevent all plunder, had their boats and stalls guarded by sentries, but this did not hinder the more daring from getting things on the cheap.

The remainder of 1810 was spent in these cantonments, with the French still in position at Santarem. 1811 brought us more fatal work.

- CHAPTER 10 -

Cazal Nova, and a Pig at Portalegre
March 1811

Massena's army of 65,000 men, progressively weakened by sickness and starvation, could not challenge Wellington's strong position around Lisbon, and in March started to retreat. Wellington's army - fully refreshed and in good health - followed.

On 6 March, we discovered that the French had left Santarem. Wellington, having received reinforcements from England, decided to follow. The enemy had taken three routes so our army divided too. Our division (the 4th), with the 1st and 6th divisions, commanded by Marshal Beresford, went by way of Thomar, while the main body went by way of Leiria and Pombal. We caught up with the French at Thomar but they saw us and retreated towards Espinal, a short distance from Pombal. They took up a strong position between these two places. We followed and combined again into one body. The French tried in vain to retain the old castle at Pombal, and slight skirmishing took place between them and some of our light troops.

At Redinha, the 3rd, 4th, and Light divisions attacked the enemy's left and, after a stout engagement, compelled them to retire upon their main body. As it was also being attacked on the right, the whole body of their army had to retreat on Condeixo. When we arrived, they retreated again, setting fire to the place, their objective probably being to prevent our cavalry, cannon, and ammunition from following too closely. It delayed us only a short time, and we marched briskly through the burning town. Condeixo must have been a beautiful little place, but after this it was one sad mass of ruin[1].

From Condeixo the French went to Cazal Nova but were so quickly followed up that Picton's division overtook them and nearly captured their leader. Next day, we faced the enemy at Cazal Nova. They were posted in a strong position on some heights and, on 14 March, the Light division attacked and forced them to retreat to a neighbouring height, where they were attacked again. Part of our division was involved in this engagement. That day I never saw cannon play so well and with such deadly effect on any body of men as ours did on the enemy, yet there were very few dead or wounded left on the field, although it was strewn with muskets and swords

- they must have carried their wounded with them when they retired to Miranda do Corvo.

At Cazal Nova, we had in our regiment a man called William Halfhead. He was misnamed for his head was so big it could have filled a half a bushel, making him the sport of the regiment. He had to have two caps to make him one. This fellow was standing within five yards of me when a shot from the enemy's cannon took the same head clean off. I heard one of the men exclaim, "Hullo, there goes poor Bushelhead." That was all the sympathy he got[2].

A division under General Cole followed the enemy as far as Panella, where it was joined by another division under General Nightingale. When the enemy saw how close we were, they retreated from Miranda do Corvo, setting that on fire too. The next time we caught up with them was on the banks of a river near the village of Poz de Aroce. It was a dark night and they were not expecting any attack let alone such a brisk one. They were driven from the river and lost more than four hundred men. It is believed that, because of their great confusion, some of those had been killed by their own side.

We encamped for one day then pursued the enemy to their post behind the river Alva. We opened fire and they retreated to Moira leaving behind at the mercy of the English and Portuguese, the 400-500 foragers they had sent out in search of badly-needed provisions. Most fell into our hands sooner or later.

We crossed the Alva on a floating bridge and halted near Moira. The enemy retreated to Celorico and Lord Wellington was obliged to stay the pursuit through lack of provisions. Soult's army had invested Olivenza and Badajoz. Badajoz was garrisoned by Spaniards, so Wellington sent our division, one of the Portuguese divisions under General Hamilton, along with a brigade of cavalry, to reinforce it. We marched southward and on 17 March, crossed the Tagus at Tancos. We advanced to Portalegre, halting there for about two days[3].

At Portalegre, an incident occurred which shows that the English often committed on local inhabitants depredations almost as bad as those of the enemy. We see other people's - and other nations' - faults yet, if light were shed on ours, they would often equal, if not exceed, those of our adversaries.

My company was billeted in a chapel. We had straw to lay on - a separate lot for every two men - which, in the morning, had to be rolled up neatly in our blankets in order to make the place look tidy during the day. Close to this chapel was a farmyard, and in that farmyard were some pigs. Now pork was a thing which the company had not tasted for some time, so we made up our minds to treat ourselves. We chose from among our number a man whose fingers were best adapted to the purpose of stealing. He took a sergeant's pike, stuck one of the farmer's pigs with it, and escaped. The poor animal wasn't long in dying and we carried it to the chapel.

We had thought ourselves unobserved, but either the farmer saw us or the pig's blood, or he discovered one missing when he counted them. He came to the chapel. He saw nothing of the pig but he could see that we were too strong for him, so he went to the colonel to report the circumstance. Meanwhile we tried to find a secure place for our prize. We thought of hiding the pig in our straw beds, wrapped in a blanket, but that would not have worked. But then we had another idea. At one end of the chapel was a large statue of the Virgin Mary. It had a robe with a long train. Under it we concealed the pig and made it look as if nothing had been altered. In came the farmer, and with him a priest. What did they do first? They paid their respects to the statue, and we watched them, trying not to laugh at the thought that they were also honouring the pig! However, it was less funny when, a few minutes later, the captain and colonel came in and ordered every berth to be examined. They searched in vain and said the farmer must have been mistaken because we could not have cooked and eaten the pig, or got rid of it, in such a short time. The farmer was still certain we had it, but he was obliged to retire without being compensated and we breathed freely at last. If we had been found out, our grog would have been stopped for a while, which is hard on any soldier.

Early next morning our kettles were at work as usual, cooking our breakfasts. That morning every man of the chapel company had an extra portion in the pot, being his allowance of the pig. After being divided among so many, we only had about a pound each, but it was something for at that time our diet was limited and we were not abundantly stocked with provision; certainly not pork. In fact, the reason for our delay on our southward march to Badajoz was the need to refresh ourselves.

From Portalegre, it took us four or five days to reach Campo Maior[4], where we caught sight of the enemy marching towards Badajoz. We encamped near a village and it was here that another shameful instance of plunder took place. I was in a foraging party of about twenty men when we arrived at the house of a poor woman who kept a kind of general shop, even though there were no other houses nearby. Four or five of us (including me) went into the shop and asked the woman if she had any bread for sale. She said there was some baking and it would be done in about an hour, if we would like to wait, which we did.

The oven was built out from the house and, at our signal, the remainder of our group set to work making a hole in the back with their bayonets. We whiled away the hour amusing the woman with some of our Peninsular tales, and when she went to draw out the loaves, what did she find? Daylight streaming in through a hole in the back of the oven, and every loaf gone!

The poor woman was in a terrible stew. We pretended to know nothing of the sad business, and did our best to reconcile her to her loss, but our pity did not detain us long. As quickly as we could we made for camp to enjoy a first rate meal off her smoking hot bread! Bread was a greater luxury than meat; we were seldom supplied with it, and never bread as fresh as this. It wasn't very well done but we would have eaten it even if it had been dough.

On the same march, I caught another cock - or rather took it from a farm-yard. I still had Tom campaigning with me and, disinclined to be troubled with another live bird, I gave it three swings by the head to break its neck and put it out of sight under my high cap. I got back to camp just as the company were falling in on parade. No sooner had the captain passed by than, much to my astonishment and his, my cap-tenant started to crow, making a terrible noise.

"Lawrence," said the captain, "what have you got there?"

"A cock. I caught it while out foraging."

"I see," he said, "you offered four, but took it with five."

I suppose he meant my fingers. He was right, of course, and I was lucky to get away with it. In the Peninsular War, many men were hanged for plunder, and at this place we were only allowed to forage for provisions for the horses and mules.

- CHAPTER 11[1] -

Grog and Sentry Duty at the Siege of Badajoz
March - May 1811

Massena's army retreated from Portugal leaving only the fortress of Almeida in French hands. On 11 April 1811, Wellington announced to the Portuguese that they were at liberty to return to their homes. He then turned his attention to the border fortresses, sending Beresford (and the 40th) south to reinforce Badajoz, and going himself to the blockade of Almeida.

From Campo Maior we continued towards Badajoz, skirmishing slightly with the enemy's rearguard with little success on either side. We halted at Elvas while preparations were made for crossing the River Guadiana, which was done on a bridge constructed of empty casks and planks. Then, about 11 April, we settled down before Olivenza, which was garrisoned by about 400 of the enemy. In a few days our batteries were ready for action. The garrison refused to surrender so we commenced firing and made a breach. Fearing an assault, the governor surrendered, and he and his garrison were taken as prisoners[2].

It was here I parted with Tom, my pet cockerel. The colonel's servant[3] pestered me, offering a dollar for him, and saying he wanted to take him to England. My comrades did their best to persuade me to keep him, but I foolishly consented. I found out afterwards that Tom had been killed for the colonel's dinner. I felt as sorry for that as I did about anything.

From Olivenza, we marched to Badajoz. It was garrisoned by Spaniards and not by the British so, by the time we arrived, it had surrendered to the French[4]. We were to invest it before its defences could be repaired so our brigade took up its position on the north side of the town and river, and started throwing up batteries.

One day, the French sallied out, crossed the river, and attempted to destroy part of our work. They engaged about 300 of our covering party until a small reinforcement of grenadiers made them retreat into the town. About 38 of my comrades died in this affray[5].

I succeeded in capturing a straggler but I could not get him into our lines because he refused to come. He kept lying down. I broke his musket but did not want to leave him, so I knelt down to protect myself from the enemy's shot and waited for assistance. The colonel, seeing my position, allowed a volunteer - Towser - to come and lend me a hand. It was a risky business for the enemy were firing at us from the fort, a short distance from the river. As the French soldier was unwilling to walk we dragged him along by his leg. The ground was so rough, he soon changed his mind, and we were able to get him to the lines at last. Towser and I searched his person and found a doubloon and a half which we divided equally between us.

The colonel reprimanded me for running such a risk for one prisoner, but I said the man might have been on the alert to fire at some of us, that he might have killed the colonel, or even me! That satisfied him for the colonel had already been wounded in the leg. He had to go into the hospital at Elvas and from there he sent a quantity of rum - about a pint each - to be divided amongst the men who had been in action at the time he received his wound. Much to everyone's discontent, the officer in charge of us - who nobody in the regiment liked - served out only half. I spoke up and said that we ought to have it all, that we had fought hard for it and the colonel meant us to have it. The officer was so put out he told me I should have none at all, but the sergeant sneaked me my half pint along with the rest. He then went to the officer to ask if I was to have any.

"Let the rascals have the lot," was the reply, "then they will be satisfied!"

So I came in for another half pint. I put it into my canteen with some water to have when I was next on sentry, which happened to be that very night, when I was commanded by the same officer.

It was not often that the major went round with the picket, but because he was standing in for the colonel, he did so that night and therefore saw me placed as an outlying sentry in a field of standing wheat. I was supposed to be relieved after three hours. It was a dark night but by the starlight I could just catch a glimpse of the enemy's fort and, owing to the heights, I was able to see the town very well. I sat down and was fairly comfortable for about an hour when the enemy started dabbing at me with musket-shots. I couldn't make out how it was they had caught sight of me and it was only after they had been firing for some time that I realised what had drawn their attention - the large, bright, brass plate on my cap was reflecting slightly either the light from the stars or the light from the town. So much for bright dress and brass plates! Fortunately, they had done me no harm and I now had a remedy. I took the loading-rod from my musket, stuck it fast into the ground, and placed my cap upon it. Then I put on my head my slop and foraging cap and went about ten yards away. There I sat down. I listened to the sound of chimes and bells pronouncing the hours of eleven, then twelve, one, two, three, and to the occasional whizzing of shells and shot over my head. I heard the bells strike four and, seeing the dawn begin to peep over the distant horizon, I knew that my turn to be relieved had long since passed. I returned to where I had left my cap. During the night, two shots had been put through it, which might have been a bit awkward if my head had been inside. I put the cap back on my head, put my loading rod back into its place, and decamped. I had seen no-one from the time I was put on sentry at night, to the moment I took myself off sentry in the morning.

The major saw me returning. He knew I should have been resting so he asked me where I had been.

"You were with the officer when he placed me on sentry last night?" I said.

"Yes. Has he not relieved you since?"

"No, so I thought it was time to relieve myself." I showed him my cap; he could judge for himself what a hot night I had had of it. I told him that I thought I had not been relieved because the officer was venting his spite for my stand over the rum.

The major was very put out. The officer had retired to rest some hours before but the major summoned him immediately and told him that if we had not been so near the enemy, he would have had him court-martialed for neglect; he would have been cashiered out of the service. It was the first and last time that officer left me on sentry all night.

While Beresford and the 40th were engaged at Badajoz, Wellington was again confronting Massena, who had advanced to try to relieve the starving French garrison in Almeida. Massena was checked at Fuentes de Onoro between 3-4 May, but on 10 May the French garrison at Almeida escaped after blowing the fortress up. Meanwhile, Soult's army was advancing on Badajoz to relieve the garrison there so, on 13 May, Beresford suspended the siege operations and moved his army to the heights of Albuera to meet this new threat. He left behind a brigade (which included 40th Regt) to guard the stores, which were destined for Elvas. On the 16 May, the 40th marched to Olivenza. There they learned that a battle was taking place at Albuera.

Beresford, hearing that Soult's army was on its way to relieve the town, had occupied the heights of Albuera, about 13 miles south-east of Badajoz, hoping to check him. General Cole advanced to Albuera as well and the action had just commenced when he arrived[6].

The Allies had taken up their position on a fine ridge of heights and, on the morning of the 16 May, the French made an attack on the right. The Spaniards who occupied it gave way in great disorder, allowing the French to gain part of the heights and leaving the brunt of the battle to the British. A noble attack was made by the 2nd division, whose 1st brigade tried to gain the ridge, but it was met by the fierce Polish Lancers who slaughtered a tremendous number of them. At one time, the battle was thought to have been gained by the French and probably would have been, had not Colonel Harding[7] hurled part of our division, and a reserve Portuguese brigade, against them thus renewing the fight. General Cole himself led our fusiliers up the hill, and was wounded. Six British guns and some colours were already in the enemy's possession, but Cole's troops dispersed the lancers, recaptured the guns

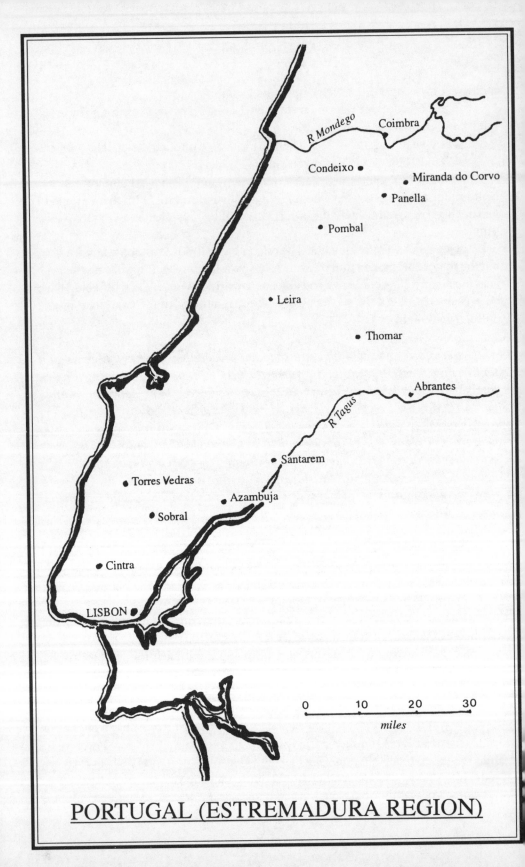

PORTUGAL (ESTREMADURA REGION)

and colours, and drove the French back down in confusion.

The Allies could not have lost less than 7000 killed, wounded and missing, while the French loss was stated to be 9000. Seldom did we arrive at a correct estimate of the enemy's loss, but the custom was to state it as being greater than ours. In my opinion the Allies lost as many in this battle as the French for, in their confusion, the Spaniards must have sustained a great loss. It was always a bother to get them to stir forward during a battle; retreating in confusion was what they were best at. At Albuera, they fired at random, and several shots went amongst the English. This engagement was sad for both parties. It could hardly be termed a victory for either side when it was so dearly bought. Still, it was we who remained on the field at the end[8].

Lord Wellington, who had taken Almeida and driven the French out of Portugal, now came southward with two divisions to reinforce Beresford's army.

Back at Badajoz, the batteries went to work again and breaches were made, but these proved impracticable. Twelve forlorn hopes and storming parties advanced into them with no better result than that many met their deaths and the remainder had to withdraw because of obstacles. As a result, the siege was converted into a blockade[9].

- CHAPTER 12 -

Fuente Guinaldo, and 'Pig' Harding's Sausages
May - December 1811

Both armies were inactive for the rest of 1811. Wellington moved the Army in the south into cantonments and encampments near the River Caza, a tributary of the Guadiana until July[1] when we were marched northward, across the Tagus, to take up a position at Guinaldo[2]. No particular engagement ensued there. The enemy fell upon another part of our line, but without success.

Lord Wellington had driven the French out of Portugal. If he had had as many troops as them he would have managed it before, and perhaps driven them out of Spain as well. He seemed to understand every move they made and was always ready to receive them. In contending with him, the French were cautious yet he only had half their numbers of dependable troops, less if some were unfit for service through want or privation - hospitals and convents could be deadly places and in them many of my comrades ended their lives, their remains carried out with no more ceremony than I described at Elvas.

The French had left Portugal in a bad state, the destructiveness of the war touching every family. Many a child was deprived of parents, many a parent had lost children, and if anyone had accumulated a little money then it was surely lost, plundered by the soldiery. It must have taken years to get over the misery and grief, if they ever did.

It must be said that, on their part, the Spaniards and the Portuguese behaved very cruelly towards the enemy's stragglers, be they prisoners or wounded. I came across one barbarous act where a ring of straw had been laid around a wounded Frenchman and set on fire. The man tried to crawl out but was forced back with a pitchfork. We fired at the Portuguese and made them fly, but the poor man's hair, fingers, and face were already fearfully burnt. He implored us not to leave him, but we had to. No doubt the Portuguese returned and killed him. He may have died of the injuries he had sustained at their hands, or perhaps from the wounds that had previously disabled him.

These barbarities the enemy brought on themselves for they dealt in the same coin. Their foraging parties, finding a whole family trying to protect their livelihoods, might kill the males, serve the females little better, and carry off everything of value. It was hardly surprising that when they were overpowered, as they sometimes were, they suffered a fate as bad as I have described.[3]

I am sorry to say that we committed depredations too but not to the extent of bloodshed. One instance was during our stay at Guinaldo. Nearly 20 of us were quartered in two upper rooms of a house where, as usual, our beds consisted chiefly of straw. The family inhabited the lower part of the house. Harding[4], an Irish comrade, was with us. We called him Pig Harding because he was always looking for, and could often lay his hand on, cheap pieces of food. He was very knowing about Spanish wiles and we had been there only a few days when, investigating with his bayonet an earthen jar containing about ten gallons of olive oil, he found about 30 pounds of sausages curled up at the bottom. They had been placed there either to preserve them, or to hide them from us.

Pig came running into our room carrying his prize and their oily state did not fail to leave traces of their whereabouts. The floor was not kept as clean as it might have been and, as our stay had hardly improved it, we made sure the stains were not noticeable. In that country sausages were generally made of cooked meat flavoured with garlic and cayenne pepper so they were fit to eat at any time and we had a fine meal off them.

"Blood and 'ounds," said Pig; "they were very good!"

And indeed they were. As soon as everyone in the house had eaten sufficient, the rest were given to comrades in another house as it was our policy to get rid of plunder as quickly as possible to avoid detection. There were always others to help eat it. In this case every sausage was gone before the woman discovered her loss, which was at dinner time the next day when, intending to make a family meal from them, she felt for them in the jar.

She guessed who the culprits were and, with her fingers dripping with oil, she rushed in crying in Spanish: "You thieves! The French are bad enough, but you are worse!" We only laughed at her so she reported us to our major and he came immediately to our room.

"Up to your prigging[5] tricks again, I see," he said. He asked the woman how much the sausages were worth. She said 16 dollars! He paid at once saying he would deduct it from our pay.

This threat had the effect of sending Pig off again in search of something that was actually worth 16 dollars! At first he was not successful, but just before we were going to move out, he found a trap-door. Hoisting himself through he found eight sides of bacon. One was all we could conveniently eat, so that was all he brought down. It was well worth 16 dollars, and the theft was not discovered before we left. As it was we heard no more from the major about our paying for the sausages, but we did not know that at the time.

Also at Guinaldo some Spaniards came into our camp with wine for sale. The wine was in pigskins, carried across the mules' backs, one on each side. Whilst a Spaniard was measuring the wine out of one skin, a hole was made in the other with a penknife, allowing both burdens to be lightened at the same time. The Spaniard was very discontented when he found out.

These activities were bad, but when you consider the frequent hungry state that such a large body of men were in during this war, perhaps they are understandable.

- CHAPTER 13 -

Ciudad Rodrigo
January - February 1812

Between 1808 and 1811, the Peninsular War had been largely defensive on the part of the Allies, but in 1812 they were ready to go on the offensive. First they had to take from the French the two key Spanish fortresses of Badajoz and Ciudad Rodrigo.

We remained in the neighbourhood of Guinaldo until the latter end of 1811[1]. The beginning of 1812 opened with the siege of Ciudad Rodrigo. We arrived at Ciudad Rodrigo on 8 January and began throwing up batteries and breastworks, being annoyed all the time by three guns which were situated on a fortified convent a little distance from the town[2]. As the convent was near to where our brigade's operations were in progress our colonel volunteered to storm it. The offer was accepted and several companies, my own included, advanced under cover of darkness. Unobserved by the enemy we took the garrison by surprise and succeeded in effecting an entrance, but the garrison managed to decamp[3].

I and a few others volunteered to march on up to the tower where the guns were situated. The path was very winding, so a priest was made to show us the way and it took at least ten minutes to reach the top. There were no French there, only three shattered cannon whose condition was hardly improved when we were ordered to throw them down. The only French left in the convent - or at least all I saw there - were two of their wounded. However they were good enough to leave us a room full of cabbages, which came in very handy indeed.

We took up quarters in the convent, but continued to build breastworks. The enemy sallied out of the town to attack us and a smart brush ensued, but they had to retire. Now and then the fortress' garrison would greet us with a cannon-ball, which did a little mischief. One killed a sergeant and took another man's arm off. I had a narrow escape myself. I was in the breastworks when a six-pounder struck the convent, rebounded, and caught me in the chest. Luckily for me it was nearly spent, but it knocked me down. It was some time before I recovered my breath and then only after my comrades poured some rum and water down my throat. My chest was much discoloured and swollen afterwards, and I was unwell for nearly a week.

By 19 January two practicable breaches had been made in the walls of the town, and an attack was ordered. Our colonel had volunteered for the forlorn hope, but it was put under other commanders, chiefly those of the Rifles. The main breach was committed to General Picton's division; the brigades of Generals Vandeleur and Colonel Barnet were ordered to attack the smaller breach. They were to be headed by a storming-party of 300 men, and a forlorn hope, under Major George Napier of the 52nd Regiment.

Between 7 and 8 o'clock, the forlorn hope assembled under the walls of our convent, which protected them a little from the enemy's shot. The business those men were about to embark on was about the worst a soldier can undertake for scarcely anything but death looks him in the face. They were silent, watching with intense anxiety for what, to many, would be the fatal signal. It came. The order to advance was given.

The assault was conducted on all sides at once and the troops were quickly at the breach, but the ladders - which were being carried by the Portuguese - were not. Nevertheless, our troops pushed onwards and gained the breach where, either through accident or neglect - and before the French were clear - a mine was sprung. French and English soldiers were blown into the air and buried together in the ruin[4]. After the smother had cleared, our troops mounted the breach and scoured the ramparts, meeting very little opposition. The French threw down their arms and retired into the town itself where, after a brief contest in the streets, the garrison surrendered.

We had been successful, but not without the loss, in the first assault, of many of our bravest men[5]. Our achievement was attended by all the horror and excess of which soldiers are capable, with riot and drunkenness taking place that night. Cellars were broke into, houses plundered of their contents, and some set on fire amid the yells of the dissipated soldiers and the screams of the wounded. In the morning order was largely restored, and those men who were sensible enough to return to their regiments, did so[6].

Besides prisoners, the enemy must have lost at least 1000 men. The Allies' loss was considerable, being 1000 also. About 41 pieces of cannon, some stands of arms, and a quantity of provisions were taken[7]. Among the prisoners were six or seven deserters from the Allied army. They were sent back to their respective regiments and probably shot. Fortunately there were none belonging to our division[8].

After the reduction of Ciudad Rodrigo, Lord Wellington put it under garrison and ordered the breaches to be repaired while he marched south to watch the proceedings at Badajoz.

We went into cantonments near Rodrigo[9]. While we were there, some muleteers, laden with biscuits and rum, halted. The rum was carried in pigskins which were easy to get at so sentries were placed over it. Instead of guarding it, they drank it, and drank so much, that they died.

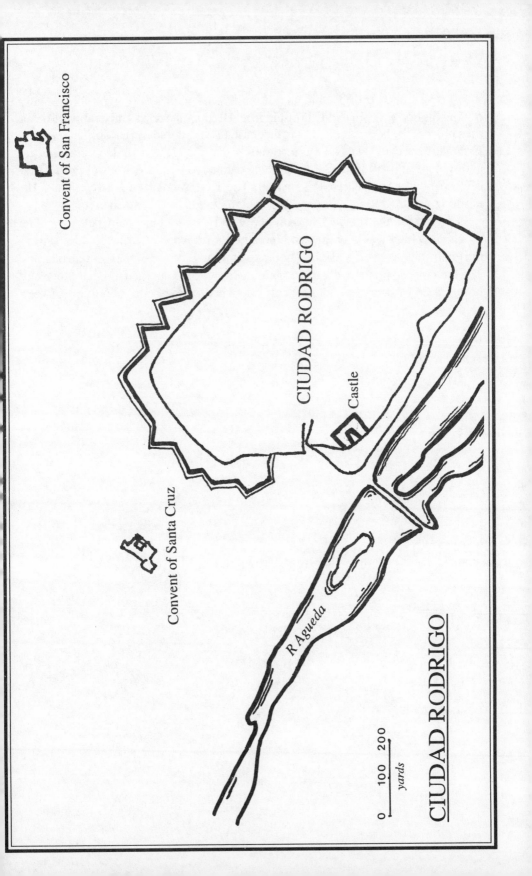

Convent of San Francisco

Convent of Santa Cruz

CIUDAD RODRIGO

Castle

R Agueda

0 100 200
yards

CIUDAD RODRIGO

It was near Rodrigo that one of our cavalry men was flogged for selfishly trading his horse's corn to buy himself grog. His poor horse was miserably thin, but then most of the horses looked like that, probably for the same reason. This was the first man to be caught and he was made an example of. He was tried by court-martial and sentenced to 50 lashes. He asked the colonel to overlook it as it was his first offence, but the colonel refused, saying: "The horse's looks tell a different tale. He has long had the bitters and you the sweet; now it is time for a change."

It is true that horses' forage, particularly in winter, could not always be procured, which was why they had more need of it when it was available. During the Peninsular campaign, the best horses seemed to be those of the German hussars. The hussars had no more chance of gaining forage than our men did, but they were not so fond of drink, which probably accounts for the better condition of their animals.

- CHAPTER 14 -

Badajoz
March - April 1812

Wellington had taken Ciudad Rodrigo, now he had to take Badajoz. The French army of Marshal Soult was tied down besieging Cadiz, and that of Marshal Auguste Marmont (who had superceded Massena) did not have the resources to tackle Wellington's army alone, despite being urged by Napoleon to do so. It was an opportune moment for Wellington to renew his efforts at Badajoz so he sent his army south to invest it again.

Our stay at Rodrigo was short and we - the 4th Division - along with the 3rd and Light Divisions under Marshal Beresford and General Picton, were ordered south to invest Badajoz, another long and tedious march of over 150 miles[1].

We arrived at Badajoz at the beginning of March and immediately began work in the trenches, throwing up breastworks and batteries. Heavy rains set in but our troops persevered. A cannonade was kept up from the town and fortunately did little damage, but on 19 March the garrison came out and attacked us. They were driven back but only after we had lost 100 men either killed or wounded. They lost more[2].

I myself killed a French sergeant. I was in the trenches and he came on the top. Like me, he had exhausted his fire and so made a thrust at me with his bayonet. He overbalanced and fell, and I pinioned him to the ground with mine. The poor fellow expired. I was sorry afterwards and wished I had tried to take him prisoner, but with the fighting going on all around there had been no time to think, and he had been a powerful-looking man. Tall and stout, with a moustache and beard which almost covered his face, he had been as fine a soldier as I had ever seen in the French army. If I had allowed him to gain his feet, I might have suffered for it, so perhaps what I did was for the best? At such times it is a matter of kill or be killed.

In case of another attack, a large number of men afterwards formed a covering party[3] for the 800 of us who were busy in the trenches every night. And still it rained. The trenches were so muddy that our shoes were covered. It poured down so fast that, in places, balers had to be employed. During the day we were employed finishing off what we had done during the night, for little else could be achieved owing to the enemy's fire.

BADAJOZ

After a few days we were within musket shot of a fine fort, situated a little distance from the town[4]. Garrisoned by 400-500 of the enemy, they annoyed us during our operations. One night, I was working in the trenches when, just as the guard was about to be relieved, a shell from the town fell amongst us and exploded, killing and wounding about 30 men. The next morning a terrible scene presented itself to us, for the remains of our mangled comrades strewed the ground in all directions. I never saw a worse sight of its kind. Some of them had their arms and legs - and what was worse, their heads - completely severed from their bodies. Working near me at the time was Pig Harding. Like me, he had become hardened to the worst sights on the Peninsula.

"Lawrence," he said, "if anyone is in want of an arm or a leg, he's got a good choice here.[5]"

The fort was very troublesome and had to be dealt with. Suspecting it had been mined, engineers were sent for. In the dead of night, between the fort and the town, they searched for a train[6]. Finding that the earth had been disturbed, they dug down, found the train and cut it off. On the next night, the 87th and 88th Regiments were ordered up to storm the fort. After a brisk action, they succeeded in gaining it, but most of the garrison escaped into the town[7].

Next morning, with the rest, I entered the fort. We saw wounded Frenchmen and relieved their pain a little by giving them some of our rum and water before conveying them to the rear. Most of their wounds - they looked like bayonet wounds - were bad, but not mortal.

Having taken this fort, we were able to carry on our works much nearer the town and, by the beginning of April, two batteries were formed within 300-400 yards of it. Within five days our twenty-four pounders had made three practicable breaches in the walls.

Lord Wellington asked the town to surrender[8]. The answer was no, so he asked that the inhabitants be allowed to leave, as he intended to take it by assault. Thousands left and he ordered that, on the night of the 6th, the town should be attacked. From each of the 3rd, 4th and Light Divisions, a storming-party was selected and assigned to one of the breaches. I joined our forlorn hope[9]. With me was Pig Harding and another comrade, George Bowden. All three of us had been quartered at Badajoz after the battle of Talavera so we knew where the shops were located. Having heard a report that, if we succeeded in taking the place, three hours' plunder would be allowed, we arranged to meet at a silversmith's shop. Pig even provided himself with a piece of wax candle in case we needed to light our way[10].

Those in the forlorn hope were supplied with ladders and grass bags to carry. We ate our rations and, at about half-past eight, fell in to await the signal for all to advance. Our men were particularly silent[11]. At last the deadly signal was given, and we rushed towards the breach.

I was one of the ladder party. At the breach, a French sentry on the wall cried out three times, "Who comes there?" No answer being given a shower of shot, canister and grape, together with fire-balls, was hurled amongst us. I lost sight of Bowden, poor Pig received his death wound and I received two small slug shots in my left knee and a musket shot in my side. Despite my wounds, I stuck to my ladder and got into the entrenchment. By now, many had already fallen, but on the cry of "Come on, my lads!" from our commanders, we hastened to the breach. There, to our dismay, we encountered a *cheval de frise* and a deep entrenchment, from behind which the garrison opened a deadly fire on us. The *cheval de frise*, was a fearful obstacle and although attempts were made to remove it - my left hand was dreadfully cut by one of the blades - we had no success. We were forced to retire for a time and remained in the breach weary with our efforts to pass it[12].

My wounds were bleeding and I began to feel weak. My comrades persuaded me to go to the rear, but it was difficult because, when I arrived at the ladders, they were filled with the dead and wounded. Some were hanging where they had fallen, with their feet caught in the rounds, and all around I could hear the implorings of the wounded. I hove down three lots of ladders, and on coming to the fourth, I found it completely smothered with dead bodies. I drew myself up over them as best I could and arrived at the top. There I almost wished myself back again, for what greeted me was an even worse sight - nothing but dead lying all around, and the cries of the wounded mingled with the incessant firing from the fort.

I was so weak I could hardly walk; on my hands and knees I crawled out of reach of the enemy's musketry. I hadn't gone far when I encountered Lord Wellington and his staff. He wanted to know the extent of my wounds and what regiment I belonged to.

"The Fortieth," I said, and told him I had been one of the forlorn hope. He enquired whether any of our troops had got into the town. I told him no, and that I did not think they ever would, because of the *cheval de frise*, the deep entrenchment, and the constant and murderous fire from the enemy behind them. One of his staff bound up my leg with a silk handkerchief and, pointing to a hill, told me that behind it I would find a doctor to dress my wounds. And so I did - my own regimental doctor[13]. I was lucky - the musket shot in my side would have been fatal had it not penetrated my canteen first, making one hole going in and one coming out.

After I arrived, Lieutenant Elland was brought in by a man called Charles Filer, who had found him at the breach, lying wounded with a ball in the thigh. The lieutenant had asked to be conveyed from the breach so Filer had raised him onto his shoulders. The night was so dark, and the clamour of cannon and musketry and the cries of the wounded so noisy, that Filer did not notice when a cannon-ball took the lieutenant's head off, so he was astonished when the surgeon asked why had he brought in a headless trunk? Filer declared that the lieutenant had had a head on when he had found him, for how else could he have asked to be taken from the breach?[14]

Poor Filer. He was hardly composed - the exposure of his person at the breach, and the effort of carrying what proved to be a lifeless burden for nearly half a mile, would have unnerved a harder temperament than his. Of course, the story spread through the camp and caused a lot of amusement at his expense. "Who took a headless man to the doctor then?" was one of the comments[15].

Lord Wellington realised it was useless to face the breach with the *chevaux de frise* so, as more success had been achieved in the other breaches, he withdrew the men from ours to reinforce theirs. He ordered the castle to be attacked[16]. For this troops were supplied with long ladders which they raised against the castle walls, but the enemy showered down on them such a mass of heavy substances - trees and large stones, and deadly bursting shells - that the ladders were broken and the men tumbled down, crushing some of their comrades underneath. There was a long delay while more ladders were procured. As soon as they arrived they were quickly hoisted. This time, the precaution was taken to fix them farther apart so that if more beams were rolled over, they would not make such a deadly sweep. This second attempt was more successful. The ramparts were gained and the French driven back. A footing was soon established for others, who succeeded in turning round some guns and firing them along the ramparts, sweeping the enemy from them. The garrison was forced back into the town. The ramparts were scoured, the breaches cleared, the *chevaux de frise* pulled down, and the main body of the English entered the town[17]. In the streets there was still some opposition, but that was soon cleared away. The French escaped to Fort San Cristoval[18].

Our troops found the city illuminated to welcome them, but it counted for nothing and they began to engage in the plunder, waste, destruction of property, drunkenness, and debauchery, that usually follow a capture by assault[19]. When the town was taken I was in camp at least a mile off but, after the sound of guns and muskets had ceased, I could distinctly hear the clamour of the rabble. The next morning, with the help of a sergeant's pike chopped up to form a stick, I hobbled into the town. There I found a pretty state of affairs!

Pipes[20] of wine had been rolled into the streets, tapped by driving the heads in, and then left for anyone to drink. To try to keep order, officers had poured away all they could. The streets therefore were running with all sorts of liquors and some men, already very drunk, lay down and drank out of the gutters.

Throughout the city, doors had been blown open by placing muskets at the keyhole to remove the locks. I saw some of our men launch a naked priest into the street and flog him down it - they had a grudge against him for the way they had been treated at a convent when they were in the town previously. I met one of my company who was wounded in the arm but said he had something which compensated him a little. He showed me a bag of about 100 dollars and said I should not want whilst he had it.

Although some of our soldiers engaged in debauchery, others did everything in their power to stop it. That morning I met many who said how sorry they were that soldiers should go to such excess, ransacking respectable houses with no regard to the entreaties of the inhabitants who had remained, and destroying what could not be taken. Men were threatened if they did not produce their money. Women too[21]. No doubt, some murders were committed. Two or three officers were killed trying to keep order and I understand that some men in the 5th division, having arrived after most places had been plundered, stole from their drunken comrades, and even killed some of them.

Not till the drunken rabble dropped into a sound slumber - or had died of their excesses - did the unhappy city became composed. In the morning, fresh troops were placed on guard and several gallows erected, but not much used. Lord Wellington punished the offenders by stopping their grog, but such scenes were not unusual after a place had been fought for so hard[22].

The garrison that surrendered numbered about 5000. 1200 had been slain in the assault, and the rest made prisoners. Nearly 150 guns, 80,000 shots, and a great quantity of muskets and ammunition were taken. Our loss was severe. Nearly 5000 of our men - including 300-400 officers - had been killed or wounded[23]. When you think of what our troops had to contend with, it was a wonder they entered the town at all that night. The storming of Badajoz was one of the worst engagements of the whole Peninsular War.

When everything was over, I remembered Pig Harding, George Bowden, the meeting we had planned, and how it had all come to nothing. Poor Pig had received seven shots in his body, and both George Bowden's thighs had been blown off. They must have died instantly. We missed Pig Harding more than anyone. He had been a thoroughbred Irishman whose jokes had helped to pass the time pleasantly, and whose roguish tricks had supplied us with many an extra piece of tommy.

I resolved never to make any more arrangements under such fearful circumstances.

The siege of Badajoz was indeed one of the worst engagements of the Peninsular War. Wellington thought the assault a 'terrible business', having known before he ordered it what the human cost would be. On the day after the storming, when he stood on the city ramparts and looked out over the carnage, he wept. That same day he wrote to the War Minister: 'The capture of Badajoz affords as strong an instance of the gallantry of our troops as has ever been displayed, but I greatly hope that I shall never again be the instrument of putting them to such a test'.

- CHAPTER 15 -

Hospitalisation, Promotion, and an Elopement
April 1812 - May 1813

A day or two after the siege, the wounded were conveyed to hospital in Portugal, some to Elvas and others six leagues further on to Estremoz[1]. It was thought that I and the comrade I met in the streets of Badajoz could withstand the longer journey, so we went to Estremoz.

At hospital in Estremoz, we were not allowed any wine or spirit. Having recently had so much of both, this was more of a hardship than our wounds. The window of our ward looked out onto a street on the opposite side of which was a wine shop and for some time its presence tormented us. The owner was often at his door looking out, and this gave us an idea. In the ward was a tin kettle which held nearly two gallons. Into the kettle we put some money then lowered it on a long piece of string down to the man in the wine shop. He took the money, put wine to its value into the kettle, and we hoisted it back up to the window. He got used to this so we were able to keep our ward supplied with grog.

The doctor, who said we shouldn't drink because it aggravated our wounds, was suspicious. He knew we had been drinking but, having no idea how we were smuggling it in, reprimanded the sergeant of the guard for not being strict in his search at the door. The appearance of our wounds did not stop us from lowering the kettle, and when the neighbouring wards got scent of the affair, it was soon going down two or three times a day!

Many in the hospital were in a much worse state than myself. Some lost arms, some legs, some died of their wounds. One of the slug shots I received in my knee could not be extricated and I could feel it, but the bone probably grew over it for it eventually ceased to trouble me.

After about six weeks I had recovered sufficiently to leave hospital, then for about a fortnight I was a convalescent, billeted at a house occupied by a widow and her daughter, who were very kind to me. When I heard that 150 of our men were well enough to rejoin the army, I asked the doctor if I might accompany them. He said 'no' because my wounds had not healed sufficiently for such a journey, but I was so sick of hospitals, physics and Estremoz, and so mad to get back to my regiment, that I went to see the captain[2], who was lying wounded in the hospital, and asked him to speak to the doctor on my behalf. The next morning the doctor said I could go, but stressed that the responsibility for the decision was mine, that he would not be answerable for my safety. About three days later, our little group started back to the army, which had moved northward from Badajoz to Salamanca, 200 miles away - a rather tedious march for men in our condition.

We reached Salamanca safely but within a few days a fever broke out and I caught it badly. I, and a number of fellow troopers suffering from a similar malady, were ordered into hospital in Ciudad Rodrigo. There the doctor had my hair cut off and my head blistered. Within hours, I was insensible, and in that state I more or less remained for three months. I was very weak but the doctor and our attendants were kind and, when I had recovered a little, I was allowed to eat anything my fancy craved. That included wine so I did not have to resort to a contrivance as I had at Estremoz.

After being in hospital another two months, I was strong enough to be moved out of town to a convent, the very convent I had helped to storm when we were throwing up batteries for the assault of Ciudad Rodrigo[3]. Others were there already, men like me who had lately recovered from illness. Amongst them were comrades from my own regiment so time passed in a more lively fashion than if we had all been strangers.

In November I was strong enough to again go on active service. I had been unfit for seven months during which time, the army - including my regiment - had been actively employed at Salamanca, Madrid, and Burgos.

The Battle of Salamanca, against Marmont's army, was fought on 22 July 1812 and ended in victory for the Allied army, whose casualties were 5000. The French lost 14,000. Wellington entered Madrid on 12 August and then besieged Burgos. This was not successful and the effort was abandoned on 21 October 1812. His army of 35,000 retreated back to Salamanca pursued by 60,000 French.

At the battle of Salamanca, our regiment had taken from the enemy a splendid drum-major's staff, said to be worth at least £50. This came in useful for our old staff - taken from the French in Holland when the Duke of York was the commander - was terribly worn and knocked about. After many long marches and retreats, they had again formed at Salamanca, to which the enemy had closely followed them. As the season was too bad to carry on the war, both sides were inactive for the remainder of 1812 and Lord Wellington put his army in cantonments. On the way the army touched at Ciudad Rodrigo which gave me a good opportunity - willingly taken - to rejoin my regiment.

From Ciudad Rodrigo, we crossed the Agueda back into Portugal to take up our winter quarters[4]. It was not a long march but it almost knocked me up. My legs did not feel strong enough to bear such marching because both of the slug shots had entered the sinew under the knee which, while we were engaged in marching, was kept constantly on the move. It wasn't until about three weeks afterwards that I began to feel more like myself, and was able to take on a regular amount of duty.

We had been in cantonments for four or five weeks and I was on sentry duty when, to my surprise, a comrade came to relieve me before my time was due. I asked him what was wrong. He told me I had been made a corporal of the 7th company[5].

My pay as a corporal was better than that as a private - 17 pence a day instead of 13 - but I did not feel at home in the 7th company where not one man stood more than 5 feet 7 inches, whereas I was 6 feet 1 inch high. Also I had none of my old comrades with me. I preferred to be a private in my own company than a corporal in the 7th so I complained to the captain and he promised that, as soon as there was a vacancy, I could go back. That cheered me up a little.

I waited anxiously for the opportunity, living meanwhile with four privates of the 7th in a private house which was close to the officers' mess-room. The landlady of our house kept a really nice pig in her sty and the sergeant of the mess-room offered her 16 dollars for it, but the old woman would not take less than eighteen. The sergeant felt that sixteen was a fair price so, instead of giving her the money, he offered it to the four men billeted with me to steal the pig. The deed was done that very night and the pig conveyed out of sight to the mess-room. In the morning, the old lady warmed the pig's breakfast as usual but found, to her surprise, that the sty was empty. She made a terrible noise about it. She suspected the sergeant. Afraid of being searched, he got some of the men to heave the pig over a wall at the back of the mess-room. The four who had stolen it got scent of this and decided that, as he had not been willing to pay the full price, the sergeant should not have the whole pig, so they went and cut off about a quarter for their own use and brought it back to our lodgings. As the old lady usually got our food ready herself, cooking the pork was a problem, but it was eventually accomplished, in our room, in a kettle borrowed from her. I had a taste of her pig. It was very good. Fortunately, she never suspected us. She was a kind lady; she had dried chestnuts in abundance and often gave them to us as a treat.

During our three months at this place[6], my captain found an opportunity to put me back into my own company. We then changed quarters, marching to an almost deserted village about three leagues off where we were cantoned, chiefly in empty houses[7]. Here there was excitement in which one of the officers of our company - a lieutenant - was the chief actor.

At our previous quarters, this lieutenant[8] - an Irishman and a Catholic - had been in the habit of visiting a Catholic chapel. There he had seen, and fallen in love with, a Portuguese general's daughter. Unknown to the girl's parents, a correspondence had taken place and meetings had followed. The prospect of our moving to new cantonments had presented them with difficulties so they decided to elope. One night the lieutenant, with two men from our company, went to the lady's house where arrangements had been made to convey her down from her window into her lover's arms, a ladder having been placed at the window, and the goods she intended taking made ready. Two Portuguese domestic servants had been bribed to carry out the goods and put them on the back of a horse, and to keep a look-out until the eloping party had got clear. However, as soon as they had received their money and the little company was on its way to the officer's quarters, they raised the alarm.

A party of six - including the two servants - was soon in pursuit and the elopement party, which was obliged to walk slowly on account of the horse being so laden with goods, was soon overtaken. The pursuers were armed with sticks, so an altercation took place. The Portuguese succeeded in capturing the horse and baggage, but the officer - backed up by his men - fought bravely for his spouse and succeeded in carrying her off. The Portuguese, one of whom had unfortunately lost two fingers in the affray, returned home content with having captured the horse and baggage.

The lieutenant got the lady to the cantonments and, on the following morning, took her to a neighbouring chapel and married her. But the matter did not rest there. The old general wrote to our colonel and said he intended to take proceedings against the lieutenant for stealing his daughter. Our colonel told the lieutenant that he should have more than marriage on his mind and that he was to consider himself under arrest. However, after a fortnight's consideration, the general relented, made it up with his new son-in-law - who was released - and gave back his wife's horse and baggage. In return for his good luck the lieutenant treated the whole of his company to a pint of wine which was drunk in toasts to the happy couple[9].

- CHAPTER 16 -

Vitoria
May - June 1813

In 1812 Napoleon was defeated in Russia from which he retreated. In Spain, King Joseph Bonaparte had dismissed Soult and taken personal command of the French army. During the long winter of 1813, Wellington prepared for a new campaign, his aim being to 'hustle' the French out of Spain.

We lay inactive in our cantonments until May, when preparations for another campaign commenced in earnest[1].

Leaving Portugal in mid-May[2], we marched in a northerly direction and crossed the River Douro[3]. Some of the difficulties we encountered in the next two weeks were almost insurmountable[4], but we arrived at last at Zamora, a town in Spain, on the north bank of the Douro, about 20 miles from the Portuguese frontier. The enemy was in occupation but abandoned the town on our approach. We followed them, first to Valladolid, about 70 to 80 miles off, and then to Vitoria, a longer march of at least 160 miles, on which slight skirmishing took place between the two armies[5]

We arrived near Vitoria on 20 June. The main body of the French were posted on some admirable heights which gave them the advantage. There was also a river which was likely to impede our progress because of our having to cross it by means of narrow bridges. We encamped. Our army was fatigued and very short of provisions so many of us set off in search of something to eat, but all I and my comrades could find was broad beans. We gathered a lot but could spend no longer than an hour at it because nearly the whole of my party were on duty that night at the general's[6] quarters in a deserted house. A kind of outhouse adjoined it and this we occupied. Stowed away inside, we found some wheat. Having also found a kettle, we lit a fire and started to cook the wheat. It made a good meal and I preserved a quantity and put it into my knapsack for a favourite comrade who had been left in camp in charge of our beans. My consideration was wasted: I discovered he had had as good a meal off the beans as we had had off the wheat! The next morning, when we fell under arms ready to attack the enemy position, we bundled the remainder of the beans into our knapsacks.

Our Division, together with the 3rd and 7th Divisions, was ordered to advance against the centre of the enemy's lines, but before we could get at them we had to cross a narrow bridge. This proved troublesome because of the murderous fire of the enemy's cannon: one shell pitched into an ammunition wagon, blowing it up along with two horses and the unfortunate driver. Once on the other side of the river, we formed into line and were up and at them. When we got near we fired and then charged them. We succeeded in driving the centre over the hill. A column of their body still appeared on our right, so we wheeled in that direction. The sight of us, and the play of our artillery on them, was enough to make them follow their centre over the hill. We pursued them, but were unable to come up with them[7].

I came across a wounded Frenchman who was crying out. A cannon-ball had carried off his thighs. He did not want us to leave him because he was afraid of the bloodthirsty Spaniards. He entreated me to stay, but I saw he could not last more than a couple of hours. Little sympathy could be expected from me. I ransacked his pockets and knapsack and found a piece of cooked pork and three or four pounds of bread. The poor fellow asked me to leave him a portion, so I cut off a piece of bread and meat, emptied the beans out of my haversack, and put them by his side. I asked him if he had any money. He said 'no', but I went through his pockets again. He had ten rounds of ball cartridge, which I threw away. He also had a clothes-brush and a roll of gold and silver lace, but I wasn't going to carry those. I found his purse at last and it contained 7 Spanish dollars and 7 shillings. I returned a shilling to the dying man and put the rest in my pocket, then I continued on my way up the hill.

There I saw a French officer coming out of a low copse close by and instantly fired at him. I did no mischief. He made his way up the hill as quickly as possible, using a sword as a walking-stick, but a German rifleman, who was on the look-out, took him prisoner. I went on with my company in pursuit of the French, who were retreating in all directions in a very disorderly state.

The uniform of the French and the Spanish was similar, so Lord Wellington had ordered the Spaniards to wear a piece of white substance round their left arm to distinguish them. The French had learned of this. In their hurried retreat, a great number of them had to pass near our lines, so they adopted the Spanish white band. We continued firing at them with muskets and artillery, but the officers saw the white on their arms and ordered us to stop. The French sunk into the valley and piled arms as if they were allies, but as soon as an opportunity afforded itself, they took up their muskets and fired right into our lines, doing terrible mischief.

I never saw men in such a rage as ours were then with the officers. I thought something serious would come of it. Fortunately, it didn't, and things passed off as well as could be expected after such an appalling mistake. If this trick had been spotted, we could have taken a whole body of French prisoners by a movement of our right flank. But the chance was thrown away, the damage done. The lives of many in our line were not recoverable; others had been injured. We took what consolation we could from watching the enemy retreat fast from where the groaning, wounded, and shattered bodies of our comrades lay.

After their defeat at Vitoria, the French left behind numberless quantities of cannon, muskets, cartridges, and all kinds of ammunition. There were also army supplies of food and clothing. Considering our need, these benefited the Allies[8]. I got myself rigged out with a new pair of boots, and not before time either. Part of the upper leathers were left on my old ones, but the major part of the sole was the one which belonged to my foot.

A shoe-wagon had been captured from the enemy and I saw that it was fast being emptied by some of our men. I asked the captain to let me fall out to replenish my shoes.

"No," he said. "When the enemy is well away, then you may do as you please."

So I had to disobey orders again, didn't I? At the first opportunity I slipped away and went back to the wagon to see what I could find. There were so many on the same errand that I began to despair of getting in, but I succeeded at last and took up six or seven pairs, throwing out about 100 pairs to the mob in the hope of making off quietly with mine. I was disappointed. No sooner was I off the wagon, than I was completely smothered by those whose craving for boots was as great as mine. I could not get clear, so I had to let the boots go and go back into the wagon for more. I got five pairs this time, threw another load out to the mob, and this time I got away, but only with three pairs.

I arrived back at my company thinking myself unobserved, but I was mistaken again.

"Disobeying orders again, are you!" the captain called out. "What are you going to do with all those shoes?"

I told him I was going to put on a pair as soon as possible.

"Very well, sir, but mind you give the rest to your comrades."

That had been my intention from the first. If it had not been, I wouldn't have troubled to get more than one pair. On marches like ours no man cared to carry a change of boots, or anything else come to that. We'd carry food, yes, for although it was seldom denied to us, it was even more seldom obtained.

At Vitoria, Bonaparte's[9] carriage had also been captured, along with some ladies that were in it. The French army had retreated to Pamplona so, under a flag of truce, Lord Wellington sent a sergeant and twelve men to escort the ladies to the French camp there. Bonaparte behaved well, giving the sergeant a doubloon and each of the men one-half of that sum, then he had them escorted out of his lines by a French officer.

Nightfall halted our pursuit and we encamped two or three miles west of Vitoria. We were there two nights and during the day we were busy foraging. Happily we found thousands of sheep abandoned by the enemy on their retreat. I was fortunate to get one and I brought it into camp. I was killing it with a bayonet through its neck when Lt Kelly[10], of our company, happened by.

"You seem a capital butcher, Lawrence," he said.

"Would you like a piece?" I asked.

"I certainly should. I'm devilish hungry."

I took out my knife and cut off one of the quarters and gave it to him as it was.

"There sir, you must skin it yourself."

He thanked me. "Never mind the skin, I'll manage that."

Several of my comrades also managed to get a share of these sheep. Our first task was to gather every odd stick we could lay our hands on - gates, doors, chairs, tables, and even window frames knocked out of the many deserted houses. It was all gathered into a heap for this grand purpose and soon mutton was being roasted and boiled all over the place! Nor had we forgotten the beans which were growing plentifully. That night we had a meal better than any we had tasted for weeks.

When it was over, we lay down. A picket was sent out in case of a surprise attack, but our comfort was not disturbed the whole night and, as our fires did not cease burning, we kept very warm as well.

Next day, those off duty again searched for food. Some returned with wheat flour, cabbages, turnips, carrots, and beans, but neither I nor Burke, a fellow-corporal, had been out. "I'll try my luck," he told me. "If the drums beat for orders, you go and get them for me, then we can share the profits of my search." I consented, and he left. He was gone for at least two hours and when he returned he was loaded. He had taken his shirt off, tied the sleeves and collar to make an impromptu sack and filled it. He must have carried his burden quite some distance for the beads of perspiration were as big as peas.

"Tare an' 'ounds!" Burke said, for he was an Irishman, "I'm tired as a dog, and hungry as a hunter, but I've got a fine lot of flour."

"Well done, Burke," I said, "we'll soon have a blow out of dough-boys and mutton."

I had taken a tin dish from a Frenchman at Vitoria and this I filled with our 'flour', adding some water to make balls of dough for the pot. It was then I saw what a mistake Paddy had made.

"This isn't flour," I said. "It's lime!" He wouldn't believe me so I told him to come and see what it looked like, boiling and smoking in the pot. He was confounded. Taking up his shirt, he hove the remainder out.

"Well I'm blessed, comrade. I'm off again, and this time I'll take good care not to come back till I have some good flour."

An hour later he returned with at least half a shirtful. Others who had been on the same scent were coming back equally well loaded. I made the dough-boys by mixing a little salt and water with flour, and put them into a kettle. The kettle was hung over a fire gipsy fashion, on two sticks placed perpendicularly on each side, with a cross-bar on the top. By night time our supper was well done. Without fat or suet, the dough-boys weren't as greasy as they should have been, but they were very acceptable in our hungry state. We had no bread, so we used some more of the mutton to help them down.

We made up our fires the same as the night before, retired comfortably, and were soon in a profound slumber.

Pamplona and Sorauren
June - August 1813

After Vitoria, the French retreated out of Spain and into the border country of the Pyrenees, leaving two pockets of staunch resistance in the well-fortified Spanish towns of Pamplona and San Sebastian. Wellington, reluctant to continue the pursuit while these towns remained in French hands, blockaded Pamplona and besieged San Sebastian. At the end of July, while he was directing the effort against San Sebastian, the French attacked the allied forces confronting them in the mountain passes of the Pyrenees.

The next day we advanced towards Pamplona. It was garrisoned by the French, so we passed it on our left and encamped near some hills with strong fortifications on their summit[2]. For a few days we amused ourselves throwing up huts as officers' quarters, cooking-houses, and the like. We thought we would be stationed there for at least 6 months, but it wasn't to be[3], and in the latter part of July we took up a position on heights in the Pyrenees. Lord Wellington had extended his army in a line that must have been thirty miles long. Our division, with a brigade of the 2nd, and a Spanish division occupied the extreme right, covering Pamplona. If the enemy had attacked any part of our line, the mountain barriers would have made it hard for us to combine. As the French were able to form in their own country, they had a considerable advantage so it was we who were running the greater risk.

Pamplona was being blockaded by the Allies and, as it was thought that Soult intended to resupply the town, Lord Wellington had sent our division to a particular pass in the mountains[4] to search for those supplies. We had marched over hills, mountains, and valleys for 30 miles before we found them - about 300 carts laden with provisions and ammunition and guarded by a strong body of the enemy. They attacked us. We gave them a strong reception and, after a severe altercation, succeeded in capturing their booty. It contained a great deal of bread, something of which we were in need, but as we were in difficult country, without a proper means of transportation, we were ordered to set fire to it. We did not want to, but the order was carried out, although not before some of our men had stocked themselves up with what they could carry. We placed the ammunition together and extended a long train, then we retired and waited. The enemy, thinking we had abandoned some of the carts, came back in force. When they were near the fatal machine, the train was fired and a great number of them were launched into the air. We hurriedly retreated back towards Pamplona, covering 20 miles in a day - hard work indeed, but no harder than a day spent in a hasty retreat, or on a well-fought battlefield[5].

The next Sunday, the troops formed a square and into it came a parson to give us a service in the field. With a drum for his books, and a knapsack to kneel on, he began to read prayers and preach when, all of a sudden, up he jumps, and to the applause and laughter of the troops, gathers up all his trappings and bolts. The cause of the sudden flight proved to be less amusing, for what he had spotted was the approach of a large body of the enemy. As you can imagine, we started running about pretty smartly ourselves!

We were soon in an action and it went on hotly till dusk. Our division lost 400-500 men. When night fell, we retreated further towards Pamplona. We were obliged to leave the wounded in the enemy's hands, but there were two grenadiers who had been shot in the thighs, and these we took turns to carry in two blankets.

We had to go through a thick wood, three or four miles in extent, which took all night. It was morning before we were finally through and we lay down like loaded donkeys. We expected to be pursued, and we were! The enemy came up and charged us hotly, making us retreat again. This time our two wounded burdens had to be left to the mercy of the enemy. In a few more hours we reached the line of our main army. I can't tell you how pleased we all were to get back![6]

Our next posting was in a strong position back on the heights of Villaba[7]. When the French made their appearance they attacked the Spanish corps on our right. The officers who should have been leading the Spanish had taken themselves out of the way leaving their men to do their dirty work, so it was no surprise that their men opened fire long before the enemy came within range, or that they decamped soon afterwards. We hastened in that direction and managed to get there before the enemy gained the summit of this important ridge. Our officers ordered us not to fire until we could make it count. The French sallied up and fired first. We returned their fire in less than a minute. In all my campaigning days, I never saw a single volley do so much execution. Almost every man in their two first ranks fell. We instantly charged and chased them down the mountain, causing more havoc. We returned to our summit and the captain[8] cheered. He praised us for our gallantry saying he had never seen a braver set of men and hoping we would always preserve our ground so well. But our enemy were brave too - two hours later they again tried to take possession of our ground, but received the same as before and were sent back down the hill.

"I think they have had enough of it this time," said our commander. "They won't make a third attack in a hurry."

But they did. Before four hours had passed they had been reinforced and were up again. Some of our men started to despair.

"We shall have to be off this time," they said to the officers who were bravely leading us on[9].

"Keep your ground if possible," the officers replied. "Don't let yourselves be beaten." We stuck to our tasks. The enemy tried to outflank us and we were obliged to wheel round to the left, but our right flank opened fire as they closed in and charged into them with the bayonet, forcing a retreat. But they came on again in support of their other companies, who were attacking our other flank. We reloaded, poured another deadly volley into their ranks then went at them with bayonets like enraged bulldogs. The fight was very bloody, but we succeeded in driving them down the mountain again.

Outnumbered about five to one we had retained our position on the heights and earned great praise from our commanders[10]. We would never have routed so many French had it not been for our advantageous ground. The whole of our 4th Division was attacked, but everyone was equally brave. Some Portuguese troops behaved very well in this action, but I can confirm that I saw no more of the Spanish that day[11]. That night we camped on the ground we had defended so well.

Our captain was as nice a man as ever commanded in the Peninsula[12]. He shared everything with the men - the rough and the smooth.

"My brave men," he said, "turn now to your fires and cook yourselves something to eat, for you have earned it."

It was an order we soon set about obeying. A quantity of rum was sent up to us and, tired as we were, we sat down and enjoyed ourselves as if nothing extraordinary had occurred. We sent out a picket but the French were not inclined to sally up and engage us again on those heights. We rested that night.

When the returns were called, our killed and wounded amounted to 74[13]. It was soon to be 75. A comrade in my company went in search of sticks to liven up our fire. I told him that if he went within sight of the enemy's picket, they might have a pop at him. He said I wasn't to worry, that he would be careful, but a few minutes later I heard a shot. I went after him. The foolish fellow had not kept to his own side of the hill, but had diverged on to the other, close enough to be observed by one of the enemy's riflemen. He had been shot in the neck.

"O corporal!" he exclaimed. "I am a dead man!"

Quickly, I dragged him back, afraid I would be shot too. When I had got him out of the enemy's reach, I took his stock from his neck. He expired immediately. I had to leave him. I rejoined our company and told them that another of us was gone.

The following morning, I caught sight of a French officer some distance away from our front lines. A fine watch-guard hanging from his pocket caught my attention and I thought how well it would look on me. More daring than wise, I crawled towards him. My musket was loaded and when I thought I was near enough, I tried a shot. All I succeeded in doing was make him take himself off and get myself into a scrape instead for I was fired at myself, the bullet taking the butt end off my musket. I turned to run off and another shot hit the knapsack on my back. I got beyond reach of the enemy's shot without any injury, but it was a close thing. When I opened my knapsack, I found that the ball had gone through the leather, through my thickly-folded blanket, and had only been stopped by the sole of a shoe. There it was, lying as flat as a halfpenny and about the same size.

Later that day[14] we were joined by the 53rd Regiment, which Lord Wellington sent to relieve us in case of another attack. They offered to occupy our heights, so that we might fall back to the rear, but our captain refused.

My men have fought well to defend their position, and I think they are strong enough to keep it, he said, and proposed that the best way of relieving us would be to keep an outlying picket so that we might get some rest. This their commander readily agreed to do.

The two armies were inactive that day, but a French officer was seen coming up the mountain. He had laid down his sword so our captain sent to meet him a lieutenant who could speak good French. The officer wanted to know if he could have the French wounded, so an agreement was made that we should take all their killed and wounded halfway down the mountain, and that they should bring ours halfway up in return, which was done. Our dead were buried, and our wounded conveyed to hospitals appropriated for them at the nearest convenient place.

On the following morning all was still quiet, but later in the day we and the 53rd were ordered to attack the enemy's position near to us, so the whole of our line was soon in motion. Acting in conjunction with the other front of our line, we drove them right off the mountains. The Portuguese troops in our division again fought well. We followed the retreating French to a village in a valley of the Pyrenees where they were delayed by a river which they had to cross. General Cole ordered up our regiment to try to stop them doing so. We pursued them so quickly there was no hope of their escape, and they threw down their arms and gave themselves up. There were about 700 of them[15].

We took their commander's gold-mounted sword, and from his cap a gold plate with an eagle engraved on it, and the regiment gave them as a present to our commander, who was a favourite because of his behaviour towards us. The prisoners were sent to St Jean de Luz to be put on board ship and taken to England.

- CHAPTER 18 -

The Pyrenees
August 1813

Throughout most of August, the French were in retreat over the Pyrenees with the Allies following closely. The 40th is recorded as having been cantoned in Lesaca from 24 August. Although events in this chapter probably occurred in August, they may have happened later (but no later than November 1813).

We marched slowly on, following the enemy so closely that we sometimes had them in sight. Both armies encamped for a week at a time and then they skirmished with one another. At one of these halts the enemy managed to get three pieces of cannon on to the top of a steep mountain. They must have been dragged up manually by ropes, because horses could not have done it. When we entered the valley, Lord Wellington was with us, and a shot from one of these cannon carried off his cocked hat.

"That was a near miss, my Lord," our colonel[1] remarked.

"Yes," was the reply, "and I wish you would try to stop them. They are determined to annoy us."

Our colonel offered to send up some grenadiers for that purpose and being a corporal I volunteered. Six other men were chosen, which made rather a small storming-party. According to my counting, the enemy numbered 26 artillerymen and an officer.

I led my little band along the valley and approached the mountain from where the artillerymen were firing at us. The cannon consisted of light six-pounders and they could not get the elevation they needed. To baffle their aim, we slowly scaled the hill zigzag fashion. Within 100 yards of them there was a slight mound on the hill and we sheltered behind this. The cannon could not touch us.

I sized them up. They had no firearms; all they had were the cannon, which were no use at close quarters on so few men as we were. For ten minutes, we lay there on the ground, trying to decide the best mode of attack while they watched anxiously for our reappearance.

At last, we were ready. "Now men," I said, "examine your flints and priming for everything must go right." I told them what to do and to make sure they acted together.

"All right, corporal," they said, "we'll follow you."

I sang out "Now for a gold chain or a wooden leg!" and we jumped up and gave them a volley. We charged before they had time to take aim at us, and so succeeded in gaining the cannon and driving the men down the mountain towards a body of infantry stationed at the foot. With my cap I signalled for our brigade to come up. They were watching and they were ready, but so were the enemy's infantry, which also started to move towards our height. Fortunately, our brigade arrived first and reinforced us. Seeing them, the enemy decamped. Luckily not one of my men was injured, whilst our volley had killed or badly wounded five of their artillerymen.

After the enemy's retreat, the colonel came up to me.

"Well done, Lawrence!" he said. "I did not think you were half so brave. No man could have managed it better."

He also praised my six fellow-stormers. A short time afterwards Lord Wellington himself came up and asked my name. I told him and he said, "I shall think of you another day."

The three brass cannon we had captured were the only ones we possessed, having been obliged to leave our own behind because of the difficult nature of our route. Even cavalry were of very little use in mountain warfare.

Soon after this daring feat, the enemy commenced their retreat again, but they only went about two miles, where they occupied another mountain. We sank into the valley. That night we slept on the ground, curled up in our blankets, as we did for many nights afterwards. We had no tents. Even if we had had, we could not have pitched them so close to the enemy. For the same reason, the numbers on picket duty were large.

Over the next few days the pattern repeated itself. We would attack, they would retreat, they would halt and make a stand, and we would attack again. There were often skirmishes between us one of which, during a short stay that we made, I was involved in.

A small body of us were out under a sergeant, an Irishman named Ryan[2], when we saw a large farm. Some of the enemy were lurking around it, so we drove them off. As we got closer, four or five more men emerged from the house and ran off. Inside was a pig which they had just killed. They had not had time to butcher it, so we started on it, but we were unable to finish the job either - a large body of French was spotted fast approaching and it was our turn to retreat.

Sharp enough work it was too! They got within shooting range and did not fail to make use of it. They chased us across a meadow which was surrounded by a very thick thorn hedge. Jumping over this delayed us terribly. I've never been much of a jumper, so I found myself in the middle and what a prickly berth it was! Sergeant Ryan had got clear and came to my assistance, He tried to pull me through and all the time the bullets were peppering the hedge on all sides of me. I was

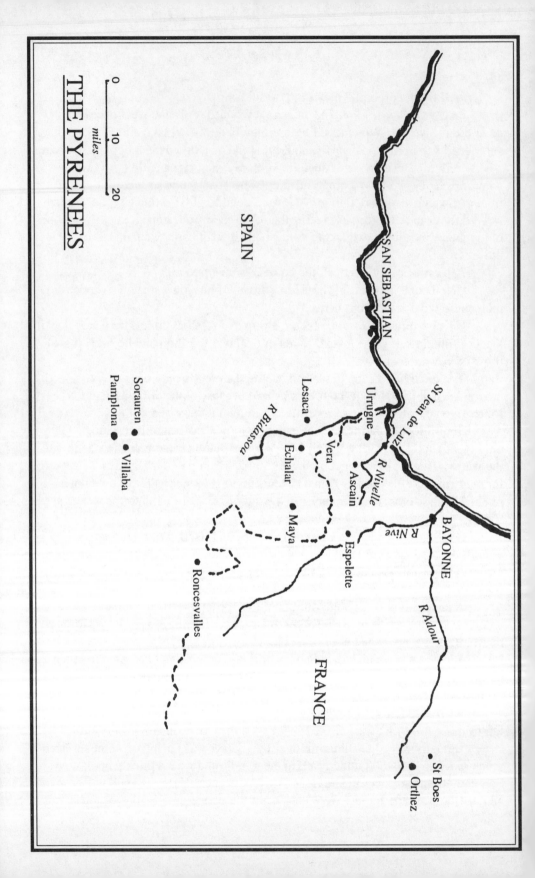

eventually extricated but I was scratched all over and had left the back of my uniform behind. We ran, but had not gone far when Sergeant Ryan was shot down. I think he was killed but the pursuit was do dogged I could not stop to find out for sure[3]. It did not ease up until we were near our own advancing lines, when the pursuers feared for their own safety. In another skirmish with the enemy's rear, we encountered about 200 stragglers, whom we engaged and drove back.

Soon afterwards, on my own and a straggler myself, I was fired at. The shot rebounded off the ground and struck the brass breastplate fixed on my cross-belt, which probably saved my life. It had come from a Frenchman lain in ambush in a thicket at the top of a mountain and he now bolted. My own musket was loaded and I could have used it, but I chased him instead. I never thought I could run so fast. I had made Frenchmen run before, but always after me! When he saw he was outdone he threw down his arms. If he had had any spirit he wouldn't have given himself up so easily. To be fair though, my musket was loaded, while his shot had been spent.

I stripped him of his accoutrements and ransacked his knapsack, but was sadly disappointed there. I took his musket and broke the stock. I did not want to be troubled with a prisoner but, as I also did not want to hurt the man in unfair play, I left him. He seemed grateful, particularly when I returned his knapsack and kit. Apart from his musket, nothing was damaged and he walked away with an air of unhurried assurance, apparently unafraid of being overtaken by any of our other men.

I ran down the slope and went in search of my comrades, who had left the mountains for the neighbouring valley. I found them in a house at the bottom, searching for provisions. As the French had already ransacked the place, all they found was a cask of sweet cider from which we refreshed ourselves. Our officer helped us out. We drank as much cider as we wanted and put the rest in our canteens. Disappointingly there was nothing to eat, for we were short of provisions and dreadfully hungry.

Our officer said we ought to be getting on, He led us half a mile to within sight of a small village, which we knew to be occupied by some French. A river lay between us and the village. There was a bridge but it was guarded by about 200 of the enemy. To reach the bridge, a long lane had to be traversed. This did not take us long but, passing through, several of our men were wounded by stragglers, or from ambush. Our firelocks were ready so we opened fire on those at the bridge, and then charged them. Although a French officer's horse was shot from under him, we were overpowered and had to retreat behind a hill a short distance away. Here we rested. We decided to attack again and, after a severe brush, we made them retreat, leaving the insignificant - but hard fought for - bridge in our possession. Our loss was fifteen whereas thirty of their men were lying dead or wounded. We pressed on for more action, firing continually as we passed through the village in our attempt to track the others down.

I sprained my foot so, when a local inhabitant asked our officer to leave a man in his house to guard it from plunder while the French were around, he chose me.

"It'll do you good to have a rest," he said.

I was quite pleased - my company was due to go back to the house where the cider had been found so I knew I was likely to get more to eat here than there! I seated myself near the door, and gratefully received the pint of wine and piece of bread the man brought me; the wine being much more to my taste than the cider had been.

I had not been there long, when I heard a heavy footstep on the staircase. I looked up. There was a Frenchman! He had gone upstairs for plunder and was coming down with a good-sized bundle of clean linen tucked under his arm. As soon as he saw me he bolted. I made a desperate lunge at him with my bayonet but he forced his bundle against it to shield himself. I had stopped the linen but I could not stop him. He made for the back door and ran out into a field. As soon as I had extricated my musket from the linen, I hobbled to the back door and sent a bullet after him. He was some distance away but I think the shot broke his arm, for I saw it drop, and his motion became slack as he passed out of sight. I went back into the house and blew the owner up for not keeping a better watch.

"Fancy letting a Frenchman find his way upstairs! He might have killed us both!" I said. Meanwhile his wife was taking the linen back upstairs as if nothing had happened.

"There is no danger of any Frenchman taking my money," the man said. "I have none." Then he gave me some more bread and wine.

I was there another two or three hours and drank the wine, but I stowed the bread in my haversack for later. I did not feel safe. There was a possibility that the enemy might fall back, so I left. I returned over our bridge to the 'cider-house'. My comrades were already there and they came and hovered round me like bees. They seemed to smell out my bread. I wasn't hungry so I divided it amongst them and it was soon devoured.

Two or three hours later the main army came up and we joined our regiment. We halted for the night nearby and our butchers started killing bullocks for our meat. Scarcely a drop of blood was wasted - we caught it all in our kettles, boiled it and ate it. It was very good. Each sergeant had to send in his return for the meat required for his company, which amounted to two pounds for each man. As soon as it was received, the cooking commenced.

The butchers, as a sort of perquisite, were entitled to the bullocks' heels, which they sometimes sold. Burke, my fellow-corporal, bought two of these for 15 pence. They should have been cleaned, the hair taken off, and then boiled, but being either too hungry or too impatient, he simply put them on the fire to fizzle. He then gnawed off the portion he thought was done, putting the underdone part closer to the fire. In that way, he finished both hocks. For a time, he seemed satisfied, but whether he ate too much on an empty stomach, or whether what he had eaten was raw and sooty, I can't say. What I do know is that he soon started to writhe in agony. The regimental doctor[4] was sent for but could do nothing. Burke suffered all night.

In the morning he was no better and, as we were ordered to follow up the enemy, he had either to march in his state, or be left behind. He chose to march. I helped him along for about a mile but then, without a word, he fell out of the ranks, lay down by the roadside, and died. I was very upset; he was one of my best comrades. There was nothing for it but to leave him and march on.

There was no contact with the enemy that day. We encamped for what we thought was one night but which turned into a fortnight[5].

At this time the siege of San Sebastian was going on. The town had been attacked twice without success so Lord Wellington ordered twenty men out of each regiment in our division to the town to act in conjunction with the besiegers[6]. When they arrived the order was given to attack. Two hours later, they had captured the town and driven the garrison into the castle, which was obliged to surrender a week later. Many died in this siege, so it was strange that every one of the twenty men from our regiment returned unhurt[7].

- CHAPTER 19 -

The Nivelle, the Nive, and another Promotion
September 1813 - January 1814

With the capture of San Sebastian in August, and the capitulation of Pamplona in October, the way became clear for Wellington to concentrate his army for the push over the Pyrenees into France. However, the weather was so bad his operations were hampered.

From early September, the 40th Regiment were at Echalar in Spain. On 7 October, with the 4th Division, they crossed the Bidassoa River, entered France, and took up a position on the height of St Barbara, from where they supported the attacks on the Great La Rhune. On 8 October they encamped again, this time at Vera where they enjoyed a month of comparative rest and where their numbers were augmented by a large detachment from their 2nd Battalion. On 10 November they took up a position on the Nivelle.

We stayed in our cantonments for about a month then again went after our enemy, with our cavalry, pontoon bridges and artillery coming on by the most convenient passes of the mountains. We often had slight skirmishes with them but no pitched battle until we came to the Nivelle, where Soult had taken up a strong position[1]. Our army halted in line, determined to attack and proceed, if possible, into France. There was nothing more to be done in the Peninsula for, on the last day of October, short of provisions, Pamplona had been obliged to surrender.

At the Nivelle, the 3rd, 4th, and 7th Divisions - under Marshall Beresford and their respective generals - occupied the right centres of the line. Early on 10 November the attack commenced with an assault on a village defended by two redoubts. Our division, under General Cole, took one of these, driving the enemy to some heights in the rear. There we attacked them again, driving them over the Nivelle this time[2]. We then went into cantonments for a few weeks[3].

The French army, however, was unsettled and unsuccessfully attacked our left. When they attacked our right (commanded by Sir Rowland Hill), Lord Wellington ordered the 6th and our division to reinforce it. By the time we arrived the action was over, the enemy defeated and forced to retreat even further into their own country, and all without our assistance[4].

While we were in cantonments, our captain - my best friend in the regiment

- rejoined us. A slight wound three or four weeks previously had caused him to be left behind, but now he was back, fully recovered. At the time our company had no sergeants. There should have been six, but they had been wounded and, probably thinking they were better off out of the smell of powder, were making no effort to get back to the regiment. The captain therefore recommended to the colonel that I be promoted. The colonel issued a written order for the purpose and I replaced Ryan[5]

I was proud of my new title and pleased to be paid 1 shilling and 11 pence per day, 6 pence more than I received as a corporal. However, as I was then the only sergeant, the whole duty fell on me.

Shortly after my promotion we were ordered to St Jean de Luz, where we received new clothes[6]. High time it was too! Our old ones were scarcely worth owning as rags and they were fearfully dirty, the red having turned almost to black. I ought to have received a sergeant's suit, but the quartermaster was obstinate and I got a private's instead. We also received a good supply of bread and rum, which was almost a luxury.

We were not in St Jean de Luz long, but were soon on another march in the Pyrenees[7]. It was some time before we encountered the enemy who were stationed in huts they had erected in the valleys. We attacked them. They fought hard, not wanting to abandon their houses in such wintry conditions, but we drove them off at last and part of our army occupied their habitations. Our regiment marched up the side of a mountain and encamped there.

We were short of provisions again and the rain fell in torrents all night[8]. We had nothing over our heads so we gathered grass, sticks and stubble and made a kind of wall to keep off some of the wind and beating rain. We tried to make up fires but everything we used was so wet that it took a long time to get them to burn, and even then they weren't very lively.

Our captain[9] asked if I could boil him a piece of beef. I said I'd try, so a corporal and myself set to work. We placed our hanger over the fire and on it we swung the kettle containing the beef, which nearly filled it. There were no springs nearby and, although it was pouring with rain, we had no tanks to catch it in. As there was only about a quart of water in the pot, it boiled away before the beef was done. The captain was impatient for his supper, so we took it up to him as it was, with the pot-cover as a dish and a wooden canteen as a plate, on the edge of which I put some salt. I had also managed to get a piece of bread, but by the time it reached him, it was as nicely soaked by the rain as our clothes were! I had a knife to give the captain but, having lost the fork, I got a stick, sharpened it at one end and gave him that instead. My contrivance was rewarded with praise.

Colonel Thornton came up and the captain invited him to partake of the beef. He was hungry and gladly accepted, so another plate, knife, and fork were needed. I borrowed the corporal's canteen and knife, and manufactured another fork for the colonel. They both said the beef was very good but not very well done, which was nothing but the truth!

The colonel sent me to the quartermaster for a canteen of rum, which is equal to three pints. When I returned, he said it was for us, so I took it to my comrade and we both sat down under our artificial wall, close to our fire, and enjoyed ourselves as much as the inclement weather would allow. We kept near our officers' makeshift 'dining-room', so that if we were wanted we would hear them call. A short time later they beckoned to us to clear away, which we did in a jocular spirit, amusing them with our remarks about wet cloths and scientific forks. They told us to keep the remainder of the beef for ourselves and we sat down to our own supper, which we were very much in need of.

After finishing most of the beef and the rum, we curled into our blankets and lay down on the wet ground to rest. The rum served to keep out the cold and wet by getting into our heads and making us feel more comfortable.

In the night the rain was torrential, completely soaking us, but by the morning it had cleared. The corporal and I consumed the rest of the beef and rum, wrung the water out of our blankets, and put them into our knapsacks. They were still damp, but we had to keep everything in readiness in case the enemy attacked which, on this occasion, happened less than an hour later. We had no baggage or cannon so, having only ourselves and our kit to lose, we retreated ten miles and halted. Expecting to be attacked again, we prepared hastily, and needlessly as it proved, for we stopped here quietly for a month[10].

During our stay, our captain had toothache and came to see me about it. "Sergeant, I am troubled with the pain. What do you advise?"

I recommended a pipe of tobacco. He couldn't bear tobacco so he took some persuading. He had no pipe of his own so I let him use mine. I gave him tobacco and he began to smoke, but not for long.

"Sergeant!" he exclaimed. "The place is whirling round! I feel precious queer! Here, have your pipe back. My tooth is better."

He gave me half a pint of rum and I heard nothing more of his toothache for a long time!

- CHAPTER 20 -

Orthez, Toulouse, and a War-Weary Tailor
February - April 1814

Inactive for most of the rest of 1813, it was not until February 1814 that we made another attack on the French, who were lying near a village whose name I don't remember[1]. We drove them over a river and there they took up a fresh position, which they left after two or three days, leaving our way clear to advance to Orthez[2].

After nearly six years of deadly fighting, we were now carrying the war into our enemy's kingdom, which was very gratifying for we were sick of Spain where we had left so many comrades lying in cold graves. Our regiment had left Ireland 900 strong and, despite having had 5100 join us from our depot since, we did not number more than 700 on our march to Orthez. The majority had been killed or wounded in battle, but many had been felled by disease, or had succumbed through drunkenness or gluttony, or had died as a result of the climate. And we must not forget the skulkers - there were many during the Peninsula campaign[3]

Portugal and Spain had long been subjected to the hateful inconveniences of war; now it was the turn of the inhabitants of the south of France. Lord Wellington had witnessed the excesses committed by the enemy on the Portuguese and Spanish and deplored them. He decided to set a better example, issuing a proclamation that there should be no plundering. The penalty? Death[4].

We arrived in France at the wrong time of year to see its beauties but, from what I could judge, it had variety. It was not unlike Spain in what it produced; there were vineyards and olive-trees, and it had oranges, pomegranates and figs.

The French took up a very strong position on a range of fine heights stretching from Orthez to St Boes. We and the 7th Division were ordered to cross a river and attack St Boes. The heights beyond were occupied by the enemy so they had a commanding view of the place. The river delayed us for there was no bridge and a pontoon had to be thrown across. Our divisions were soon over it. Joined by a brigade of cavalry and artillery, we formed line and marched on St Boes.

The village was stoutly defended by the enemy, who fired briskly at us and stood their ground for a long time, but troops of the 4th Division, under General Cole, poured in on them like lions and they were eventually forced to take refuge on the heights. We followed, but the ground was to their advantage. The heights were formidable; nevertheless, we rushed up them, only to be driven back again and again by the fearful play of artillery. Their position was only accessible in a few places, and those places so narrow they would admit only a small body of men at a time. Despite all these disadvantages, our men - strongly reinforced - carried the heights. The rest of our army had also succeeded in driving the enemy from their lines, the cavalry pursued them, and many prisoners were captured. Some field-pieces were also taken[5].

The enemy fell back on the River Adour, and then took up another position on heights near the town of Tarbes, but were forced to retreat from there, first towards St Gaudens and then to Toulouse on the Garonne. There, on the right bank of the river, on more heights, with every assailable part strongly fortified, they again stood on the defensive.

Our march was difficult. The bridges which had been destroyed had to be replaced with pontoons, and those that remained were strongly fortified. One of these bridges was guarded by some French cavalry, and we annoyed them considerably with our fire as we approached. Behind us was a ditch so we knew we could fall back to it for protection if they attacked us. We also knew that a body of hussars was waiting out of sight, ready to fall on them if they moved against us. Armed with such knowledge our fire was daring and we enticed out a body of about 300 horsemen. They crossed the bridge under our retreating fire, but when they got close, we fell into our ditch, and our cavalry came up. Some close shaving ensued and soon a large quantity of spare heads, arms, legs, and a good many horses were strewn over the ground[6].

The enemy were tumbled back over the bridge, and when our division came up, we followed them to their heights, keeping Toulouse some distance to our right. Before we reached them we had to attack and carry a small village they had occupied. This was the commencement of the action of a bloody day which cost the armies on both sides many of their best men. It was fought on Easter Sunday 1814[7].

From the village the ground was difficult but we formed line and dashed up the hill to attack their right. All the while we were under fire from their artillery, which was so brisk that one of General Cole's orderlies had his horse shot under him. The hill was defended by thousands of the French, half of them cavalry, and their fire was a perfect storm of grape and canister, which we returned[8]. Directly we got near, we started to charge them but on the appearance of their cavalry, we halted and formed squares. The combination of their infantry and cavalry would have routed us had it not been for the Rocket Brigade, which played havoc with their cavalry. It was the only time I saw a rocket charge and it was most successful, for it soon turned the enemy about.

The Spaniards were engaged on our right, and I never saw them fight better. They suffered more than the British because the French, knowing them to be cowards, pressed hard expecting success in that quarter. But this time they were as determined as the British; they stood their ground well, and only a few of their number got into confusion.

As soon as we had gained the advantage and taken part of the heights, our artillery joined us and the combination forced the French to fall back to their works at Toulouse. We camped on our newly won heights overlooking Toulouse.

Fighting at Toulouse had been a man called William Marsh, who was in my company. A native of Bath in Somerset, he was a tailor by trade and had earned many a shilling from those of his comrades who employed his skills. He had joined the army for seven years. That period had expired and although he was desperate to get away from all the conflict and bloodshed, owing to the continuation of the war, he had not been allowed to leave. There were thousands of others in this plight, several in my own company. Sixteen guineas had been offered to each for their services for life and many had accepted, but among those who had refused was William Marsh. He was so sick of war that, before the fighting at Toulouse, he wished both his legs would be shot off so that he might be out of the affair altogether. When a musket-ball took him sideways and pierced the calves of both his legs, he sang out heartily, and I couldn't help saying: "Hullo there, Marsh; you are satisfied now your wish is fulfilled, I hope?"

He begged me to move him out of the thick of the fight, so I dragged him under a bank and left him there. I never saw or heard anything more of him. It was far from being a mortal wound, but neglect may have turned it to something more fatal[9].

Another comrade was in the front of our line when a cannon ball pitched onto his foot and smashed it. He somehow managed to hobble to the rear on the heel. I felt sorry for him. He was a brave soldier, and seemed to be enduring great agonies.

When night drew in, all firing ceased, and when we looked around for firewood, I came across a Frenchman. Badly wounded by a shot in the stomach, he had crawled under a bank. I asked him if I could do anything for him. He asked for water. My canteen was nearly full so I gave him some. He drank heartily, but it fell out again through his wound. He pointed out a house about half and mile off and told me it was his father's. I was astonished! He hadn't seen his parents for six years. Since his return to the area, he had not been able to fall out and visit them. He begged me to take him there so that he might die in their presence, but I told him I could not because the French were there. What I did do was get an old blanket and wrap it around him, and make him as comfortable as I could in the circumstances. He seemed more resigned to his fate and I left him.

I ate my supper, drank my allowance, wrapped my blanket around me and slept. I woke early next morning, put my things straight and, having nothing particular to do, went - out of curiosity I suppose - to see if the Frenchman was still alive. He was cold and stiff; he had died some hours before.

The loss to the Allies in this action was over 4000 killed and wounded, 2000 of which were British. The enemy's loss was 3000, but they had had the advantage of the ground and we suffered from the artillery before we were able to return a shot[10].

Toulouse would not surrender so Lord Wellington ordered fortifications to be thrown up ready for the reduction of the place. They weren't needed - in the dead of the night the French disappeared and retreated in a south-easterly direction towards Villefranche. Although we followed, and part of our army had skirmishes with them, we never again saw their main body for, a day or two later, news came that Bonaparte had been overthrown and that peace had been proclaimed[11].

This was good news for most of our troops. It may have taken away from the young officers their chances of promotion, but it made death less likely too. Ambition can lead a man a long way off course and add tenfold to his sorrow.

Things now assumed a different aspect. Everyone was in a joyous state especially the Spaniards, who had always been ready to give up fighting. We encamped for few days more[12] and were then ordered to Bordeaux where we were to be shipped back to our isles. The Spaniards and Portuguese were to be sent back to their own country. The Portuguese had been the better race in the field of action, but they too were happy to be returning to their own country, pillaged though it was. Before we left, I had long conversations with stragglers of both nations.

(*Above*); The Storming of Monte Video, February 3rd 1807. British troops move forward in the darkness to storm the breach in the town's walls. (*Below*); The death of Captain Renny of the 40th Regiment, who was shot dead as he reached the top of the breach at Monte Video.

(Above); The Battle of Talavera, July 27th-28th 1809. *(Below)*;The Battle of Bussaco, September 27th 1810. Marshal Reynier's attack upon that part of the Allied line held by the British 3rd Division.

(*Above*); Allied troops file into the Lines of Torres Vedras in late autumn of 1810. (*Below*);
The British Army fording the Mondego river in pursuit of Massena's army in the spring
of 1811 following its withdrawal from its positions in front of the Lines.

(*Above*); 'Saving the Colour at the Battle of Albuera, May 16th 1811.' The 3rd Regiment (The Buffs) fight to hold off Polish lancers during the battle. (*Below*); 'A View of the Siege and Storming of Ciudad Rodrigo in Spain on January 19th 1812'. An old print showing the storming of the town.

(*Above*); 'Badajos on the Guadiana, as approached from Albuquerque and Elvas'. The town as seen from the left bank. On the extreme left can be seen the high walls of the castle.(*Below*); 'Badajos Taken by Storm on the 6th of April 1812 by the Allied Army under Lord Wellington'. British troops move forward to storm the breaches at Badajoz.

(*Above*); Wellington inspects the breaches at Badajoz on the morning of April 7th 1812 following the successful but appalling and bloody storming of the place the previous night. (*Below*); The centre of the British Army at the Battle of Waterloo, June 18th 1815. British infantry squares under attack from French cavalry close to La Haye Sainte.

(*Above*); The Battle of Waterloo. Wellington encourages the hard-pressed British infantry squares as they await another French cavalry attack . (*Below, right*); An Officer and Private of the 40th Regiment of Foot, 1815. (*Below, left*); William Lawrence's grave at St Nicholas' churchyard, Studland.

(*Above*); Studland, about 1888. The building on the right is the 'New' inn, now the Bankes'
Arms. The cottage on the left was the 'Old' inn, ie Lawrence's 'Wellington Inn' and
(*Below*). George Bankes' Manor House, now the Manor Hotel, Studland.

- CHAPTER 21 -

Peace and Plenty
April - June 1814

The treaty of Fontainebleau, which granted Napoleon two million francs and allowed him to keep the title of Emperor, was ratified on 16 April. It was reported that, as he left Fontainebleau, Napoleon murmured that the violets would be back in the spring, and so would he. He sailed to exile on the island of Elba on 28 April. Louis XVIII was restored to the throne of France, and Wellington was offered the post of Britain's ambassador in Paris. The Peninsular army was directed to go to Bordeaux for dispersal.

It seemed we were in no hurry to quit France. We were often billeted at towns and villages longer than necessary so, although it was comfortable, our march took a long time to accomplish[1]. The best billets were chosen for the officers, then for the sergeants, and then for the corporals and privates. The numbers were matched to the accommodation available, but I seldom had more than one other person sharing with me.

The inhabitants could not have behaved better if they had been our own countrymen, and just before arriving in Bordeaux, myself and a private found ourselves in clover when we were billeted at a gentleman's house. Fortunately, we were staying from the Saturday night to the Monday morning.

As soon as we arrived we were shown to our room, which was beautifully furnished. When we had taken off our accoutrements, we were taken downstairs to a sort of bath-room, where tubs of water had been placed in readiness. We had a good wash in them. Back in our room, we made ourselves comfortable, with the gentleman sending up clean stockings, a loaf of bread and a large bottle of wine, containing about three pints. This we found most acceptable. When the family's dinner was ready, our hostess insisted on our dining with them.

I wasn't used to pomp, being more accustomed to the kind of dinners and suppers our colonel and captain had recently taken part in, so I would have got out of the invitation, but we were pressed. We were shown into the dining-room and sat down with the lady and gentleman.

I had never seen anything like it for the table was laid out gorgeously. The silver was glittering but awkward in our clumsy hands, used as we were to eating with our fingers. The dress of the waiter, who was probably the family footman, was fine and ugly, and his hair was plastered with the white powder to which I had taken such an aversion in my early days in the army. The dinner was good and I freely partook of it, although I had little idea what I was eating. Some good wine was handed round, and our glasses were constantly filled.

After dinner, we were surprised when the white-haired waiter entered with coffee. More as a compliment than because we needed it, we took a cup each with some sugar-candy to sweeten it. The gentleman asked if we smoked. We said yes, so a bell was rung and the footman entered with tobacco. The lady retired into the drawing room and we took a pipe with the gentleman. We were used to the Spanish language, but not to French so we were unable to understand half what the gentleman said. The wine made us chatty anyway and we thoroughly enjoyed ourselves with our pipes. We began to feel new men in all our grandeur and were quite getting used to the distinguished style!

We were next invited to take tea in the drawing-room, but we were so tired we begged to be excused. This was granted and the bed-candles were rung for. We wished the gentlemen good-night, went to our room, had a hearty laugh over the evening's business, then retired to rest. Our berth was a fine feather bed, a luxury we had not seen for years. In fact, it was such a luxury that it was too soft for our hard bones.

My comrade jumped out of bed. "I can't sleep here!" he said.

"Nor can I," I replied so, with a knapsack for a pillow, we wrapped ourselves into a blanket, lay on the floor, and sank into a profound slumber.

We overslept. It was late in the morning when the servant knocked at the door and said breakfast was ready. Soon after, the master himself came up. He knocked and we called for him to come in. When he opened the door and saw we had been sleeping on the floor, he wanted to know if there were fleas in the bed! We tried to make him understand what had happened. He went back down and we followed soon after. An excellent breakfast was waiting. Our hosts finished before us and left.

After breakfast, the servant entered and conducted us to the drawing-room. It was splendidly furnished, but for my own part I would rather have been down in the kitchen. We went in and our hostess, anxious that we should understand one another better, took down a book describing the French and English languages. She asked us why we did not sleep on our bed. We told her we had not slept on a feather bed for six years. She had other questions and I answered them, giving some idea of the trials a soldier went through in time of war. She was so touched, she started to cry, particularly when I said that, as an example to the regiment, two privates were to be whipped that very morning for being drunk over-night and causing a disturbance in the town.

It was a Sunday morning and the drums beat for assembly in the town square where the punishment was to be witnessed by the regiment, and by the inhabitants.

We joined them. The two men were brought in and their sentence of a 100 lashes each read out. Then the first man was led to the halberds. Before the drummers could begin, five or six gentlemen of the town made their way into our square and begged the colonel to let the men off. They said it was the wish of the inhabitants. The colonel was persuaded and dismissed the victims with a reprimand. The two men thanked the colonel; he told them that had it not been for the timely interference of the gentlemen, he would have given them every lash.

We were ordered to disperse, and I returned to my excellent quarters where, for the rest of the day, we again received no end of kindnesses in the way of luxurious meals, and coffee, and plenty of wine. Before we went to bed, brandy was introduced to finish off. We took a glass of that with hot water and then retired, sleeping as we had the night before.

We had to assemble at 7 o'clock the next morning. As there was no time for breakfast, our host ordered our canteens to be filled with his best wine, and a parcel of sandwiches was made up for us both. We shook his hand, thanked him for his hospitality, and rejoined our regiment, which now headed for Bordeaux. It was no more than a day's march away so we reached it the same night.

We encamped on the banks of the River Garonne[2] - down which even large ships could ascend - two miles from the city. We were there five or six weeks and every day, swarms of costermongers visited and sold us wine, spirits, bread, meat, fish, and fruit of every description. Often on a Sunday, the inhabitants of Bordeaux would make excursions to inspect our army. Every Sunday the regimental bands played, and the French danced. Many of them - male and female - were on stilts, which we found very entertaining. And there were other kinds of other jollities, in which our soldiers freely joined[3].

It was at this place near Bordeaux that no fewer than seven of our company sergeants reappeared. Fearing abandonment in some foreign country, they had left their snug dens, and their trivial employment - as doorkeepers or wardmasters in the pay of the Spaniards or Portuguese - to rejoin us. Some, like myself, had indeed been laid up at Elvas and Estremoz, but it had been their duty to follow up the regiment as soon as they were able, as I had done. Two had been hospitalised on our retreat from Talavera, and had not shown themselves since. The others had been away similarly, but for shorter periods.

Apart from the time he had spent in hospital, our company captain[4] had, like me, been through the whole campaign so when the sergeants returned he pretended not to know them.

"Where on earth have you come from?" he asked. "From the looks of you you don't appear to belong to my company." He called me over and asked if I knew them.

"They seem to have been in luck's way about their clothes," I remarked. And so they did. Ours were as ragged as sheep and as black as rooks with the captain's as bad as any private's, but theirs were red and as new as if they had never been on. It was the same with their shoes. Ours were completely worn out by our continual marches.

Now they had all returned, our company was overstocked with sergeants, having two more than our complement of six. Our captain solved the problem by sending to the colonel the two who had been absent the longest, with a written request that they be transferred. The other five he allowed to remain, but only for a short period. He told them his company should not be disgraced by them any longer than was necessary and that many of his privates deserved the stripes more than they did.

- CHAPTER 22 -

New Orleans and Dauphin Isle
June 1814 - May 1815

After five or six weeks, our army embarked onto ships bound for various parts of the British Isles[1]. Our conveyance was the *Sultan*, a fine man-of-war with 74 guns, and its sailors had a good laugh at our ragged appearance.

As most of our regiment were Irish, we were again despatched to Ireland. We had a good passage, landing at Monkstown near Cork[2]. We marched to barracks in Fermoy and after two or three days there were transferred to Athlone in West Meath where we were stationed for about two months[3].

The Peninsula trip had lasted six years and although money had been advanced to us at various places, there had been no proper settlement. While we were in Athlone, the accounts were made up. Some of our sergeants received as much as £50 or £60. As one of the younger sergeants, my own lot amounted to £40. The regiment was granted a week's furlough and, not having been in the British Isles for so long, we were resolved on having a spree. Most of the money probably melted away in that period; I know mine did, even although I slept in barracks in Athlone every night. What duty there was, the militia were ordered out for.

I would have liked to have gone to see my parents, but the furlough was so short I didn't have time to cross the Channel. However, I wrote to let them know where I was. Parents, no matter how rackety, always worry about their children. I had written from the Peninsula too because I knew they would worry when they heard, or read, about the scenes taking place there.

The peace did not last long. We were again ordered on foreign service, and marched to Mallow in Co. Cork[1]. There we were joined by our 2nd battalion and all in that who were fit for service were drafted into our battalion. It was here that our captain got rid of the remaining skulkers. He left them behind in the 2nd battalion, which annoyed them, replacing them with braver men, choosing from among the privates who had distinguished themselves in conflict. We went onto Cork and then to the Cove, where we embarked for the West Indies[5].

In Ireland for only three months, we had scarcely slipped out of one war before being launched into another. The unhappy scenes of parting that had taken place at Portsmouth were repeated, but were soon forgotten when we set sail.

On leaving Cork Harbour[6], a terrible gale blew up and we had to put in at Bantry Bay. One of our ships was lost on the rocks and although all on board were saved, they lost their equipment[7]. They were taken on board various ships and, as soon as the weather turned fair, we returned to the Cove and waited three weeks for fresh supplies. When they arrived, we set sail again, amusing ourselves on the voyage as we best could. The weather was good so we arrived at Barbados as soon as could be expected and there anchored for a short time[8].

Before we sailed for the West Indies, one of our captains had sold his commission to a younger officer for £1200. On that first night, this young man went ashore and slept there. He caught a fever, was brought back on board, and within a few hours was a corpse. The disease was infectious so he was immediately sewn into a blanket with two of our large shot and put into the sea. With no minister on board, the funeral service was read by an officer.[2]

From Barbados we sailed to Jamaica[10] and anchored off Port Royal. It was here a girl was discovered on board. Unknown to the captain, some sailors had smuggled her aboard at Cork and concealed her in a bundle of straw. Port Royal was the best place for shipping her back to England. I was sergeant of the watch, so I and two privates were called upon to take her on shore. We took her to a kind of public-house. The people there were all blacks and they were dancing to their own rough music, even although it was two o'clock in the morning. We asked for the landlord and he appeared from among the company. He was as black as a crow and was steaming from the dance. I inquired if the girl could have a bed for the night. He said, Yes, for a dollar, which was a stiffish price considering it was already two in the morning! I paid him anyway. The unfortunate girl was broken-hearted. I felt very sorry for her but, under the circumstances, there was no more I could do. We left her and returned to our ship. I hope she got back safely to England.

After a week had elapsed, a gun-brig[11] arrived to convey us to North America, England then being at war with the Americans.

Relations between Britain and America had been strained ever since the American War of Independence. The Americans had resented the measures taken by the British in support of their war effort against the French, eg blockading American ports, and preventing neutral ships from entering French ports. Hostilities broke out in June 1812 when American forces invaded British Canada. The Americans were repulsed but not before they had set fire to Toronto. The following year, the British retaliated by sending an army of 4000 Pensinsular veterans to set fire to Washington. A peace was eventually negotiated and signed at Ghent in December 1814, but as news of it did not reach America until February 1815 the war continued unabated. In December 1814, the army of Sir Edward Pakenham - Wellington's brother-in-law - was ordered to assault New Orleans.

New Orleans, in an almost impregnable position on the bank of the Mississippi, was defended by General Andrew Jackson. Pakenham's batteries started shelling the city on 1 January 1815. The main assault was on 8 January. The

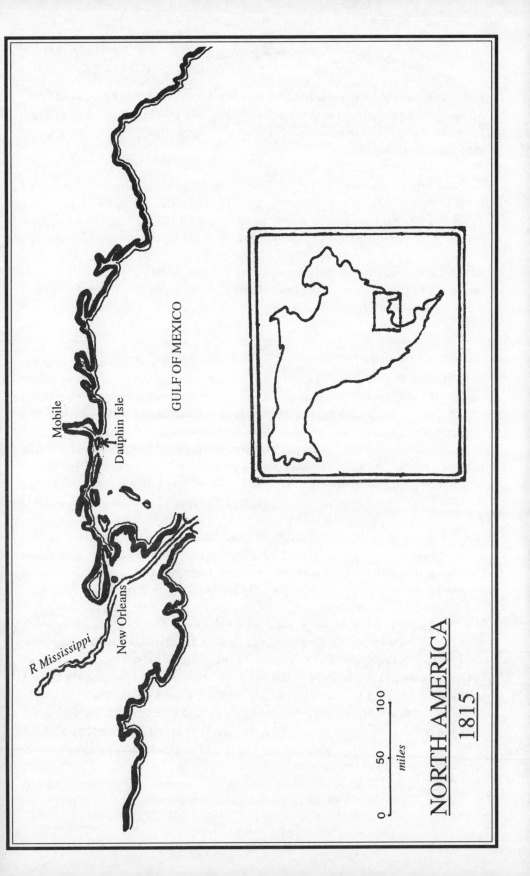

R Mississippi

New Orleans

Mobile

Dauphin Isle

GULF OF MEXICO

NORTH AMERICA
1815

0   50   100
miles

ships carrying the reinforcements (which included the 40th Regt) anchored in the Mississippi on 9 January, and the next day the men - unaware that the action had already taken place - were ordered into smaller boats to be taken 80 miles up the river to New Orleans.

The gun-brig carried us to the mouth of the River Mississippi where we transferred to barges which held about a 100 troops each. These were towed up the river by other small sailing and rowing boats. Our force consisted of five English, two black regiments[12], and a battalion of marines. We were put on shore near Orleans.

Although the boats which had been carrying the 40th and the other reinforcements up the river to New Orleans were ordered to return to the fleet, two or three reached their destination and it would appear from his account that Lawrence was in one of them.

That day, we marched to Orleans and encamped about two miles from the city. During the night we skirmished with our new enemy but without major casualties. Next morning, we advanced in a body to attack a battery constructed chiefly out of barrels of brown sugar[13]. At first, we were warmly received with the cannon and musketry of those planted there, but they soon got tired of our Peninsular medicine and retired into the city. There was no more fighting. Apparently terms had been agreed, so when the black regiments had eaten a quantity of the battery fortification (of which they seemed fond), and we had put some more into our haversacks as a sweetener for our cocoa, we returned to our boats.

Pakenham was defeated on 8 January. He and 2000 of his men were killed, but his army remained outside the city. Maj Gen Sir John Lambert, who had taken command, decided to abandon the operation against New Orleans and re-embark his troops, which was done under cover of darkness on 18 January.

We went down the river to a piece of land called Dauphin Isle, where we encamped[14]. Apart from alligators, racoons and oysters, the island was uninhabited. We had plenty of provisions in the form of meat and flour, but we had no bread because we had no ovens, so we set to work constructing one. From the vessels we received a lot of iron hoops and these we formed into an arch. By burning oyster-shells we obtained lime and by mixing it with sand and water made some very good cement. That was how we constructed our oven and it baked as well as any English 'one, considering the type of dough we had. It answered our needs so well that at least twenty more were constructed on that once desolate, but now busy, little isle[15].

On the coast we were always looking for oysters, which were there in abundance. Those who were more industrious collected them to sell to the troops who preferred buying to gathering, or who were unable to go on the sands themselves because they were on duty. The oysters were very cheap. Half a bushel might go for one dollar, which wasn't much when you consider how much trouble they were to collect.

A playhouse was also erected and some of the cleverer officers and men used it to amuse the troops. The scenery was rude but with these, and other games, our three months on that island passed quite pleasantly[16]. It was winter and the poor blacks suffered so dreadfully from the cold that they were sent back to their own country long before we left.

When the order came to return to England, we were overjoyed. It had been a short campaign compared with our Peninsular affairs, but we weren't sorry for that. We embarked on board the same ships[17], and tacked to the West Indies to get provisions. At one of the Spanish islands[18], we took on water and live cattle, and for their feed there was a kind of cabbage which, on account of their size, were called cabbage-trees.

Our destination was Portsmouth and it was a pleasant voyage with fair weather prevailing[19]. When we neared England we encountered an English frigate and were informed that our old enemy Napoleon Bonaparte had left the island of Elba and, with a small force, had landed in France where he was collecting more troops - 100,000 of them.

This was disappointing news for if Bonaparte intended disturbing Europe again, we would have to go back. It caused quite a stir on board among the young officers who, ravenous for promotion, rejoiced at the news and treated all the men to an extra glass of grog in order to make everyone as lively as themselves.

When we were near Portsmouth, a signal was raised for us to go to the quarantine area. A yellow flag was hoisted for a doctor to come and inspect us on board. He found all to be in very good condition. This was reported to the general, but we did not set foot in England. Instead, the very next morning[20], we were signalled to weigh anchor. We were going to Flanders.

I left Portsmouth with a lighter heart than I had the first time for I was now more used to war and hardships than to peace and plenty. Even so, I would have preferred not to go on this errand.

- CHAPTER 23 -

Waterloo
May - June 1815

On 26 February 1815, Napoleon left Elba with a small force of 1200 soldiers. He landed at Provence on 1 March and marched to Paris, entering on 20 March without a shot being fired in anger. Louis XVIII, whose popularity had been on the wane, had fled to Ghent the night before.

On 25 March the formation of an alliance of European powers to combat the renewed threat from Napoleon was announced. Wellington was appointed Commander-in-Chief of British, Dutch and Belgian forces in Flanders. He arrived in Brussels on 4 April to take command. British troops were despatched to the Netherlands and, as they arrived, were deployed to the west of Brussels, the Prussians being deployed to the south.

By 14 June Napoleon had an army of 122,000 men massed around him at his headquarters in Beaumont, on the border with Belgium. The Anglo-Dutch and Prussian forces numbered 210,000, therefore Napoleon's tactic was to divide them. He made his move on 15 June, and on the 16th his army battled with the Prussians at Ligny, while the French army of Marshal Ney fought the Anglo-Dutch (led by Wellington) at Quatre-Bras. The Allies held out at Quatre Bras with losses of 5000, the same as the French. The Prussians fared worse against Napoleon, losing 15,000 to the 12,000 French casualties. The Allies retreated and formed into one body to defend Brussels. The place chosen was south of a village called Waterloo.

Our voyage was a short one, lasting only a day. Early in the morning we were within sight of Flanders and there we anchored. Small vessels came alongside and conveyed us to the quay at Ostend, where we came ashore[1]. We marched half a mile to a canal, where we embarked on large open barges which were towed by horses. We passed Bruges, about 12 miles from Ostend, and carried on to Ghent which, at a rough guess, was twice the distance. We landed at Ghent and were there about nine days. Louis XVIII was there too. After a reign of ten months, Napoleon had obliged him to flee Paris[2].

At the end of the nine days the drums beat at midnight, and we arrayed ourselves in marching order. The landlord of the house in which I had been staying got up and insisted on filling our canteens with gin. He gave each of us some bread and meat, and warned us to look out because the French were coming. When everyone was assembled at the rendezvous, orders were given to march straight to Brussels. I don't know exactly how far it was; probably not less than 40 miles, but it took two days of hard marching[3] to get there.

On 17 June 1815, we marched through Brussels. The inhabitants were joyous and brought out all manner of refreshments. Some remarked that we were going to be slaughtered like bullocks, but we laughed and said that was nothing new. Some of the younger recruits were very frightened at the thought of fighting, yet in battle it was often the timid ones who rushed forward and got killed first. Disciplined soldiers know better.

We marched about five or six miles out of Brussels and were not far from the village of Waterloo when our commander sent his aide-de-camp to Lord Wellington to find out at what part of the line we were to fall in. We were ordered to stay where we were until morning, so that night we sheltered anywhere we could find - cowsheds, cart-houses, and all kinds of farm buildings. There never was a worse night - the rain was torrential and the fearful thunder and lightning were a forewarning of what was to happen the next morning, which was again a Sunday.

On the 16-17 June, the allied army had been attacked at Ligny and Quatre Bras by Napoleon's large force. Neither side had obtained an advantage despite thousands being killed. Firing was still going on, and on the night of the 17th I could hear it distinctly, in spite of the thunder. All through the night too there was the clamour of thousands of camp-followers who, fearful of sticking to the allied army after Quatre Bras, were retreating to Brussels with a stream of baggage wagons. It was quite a sight. The roads were almost impassable and some people got stuck in the mud.

Early in the morning we marched to join our lines in the reserve, alongside the 4th and 27th Regiments and a body of Brunswickers and Dutch[4]. Between us we formed a line between Merk Braine and Mont St Jean on the Brussels road. Our regiment took the left of the road but we were not there long. The French could be seen in motion and when they opened fire with their cannon, we marched up to the action in open column.

During this movement, an enemy shell cut our deputy sergeant-major in two, then went on to take off the head of William Hooper, one of my grenadiers. It exploded in the rear no more than a yard from me, the impact hurling me six feet into the air. The tail of my sash was completely burned off and the handle of my sword was singed black, but fortunately the only injury it did me was to take a small piece of skin off the side of my face. Another narrow escape.

"This is sharp work to begin," I said to a sergeant who was standing close to me when I fell. "I hope it will end better."

This event frightened Bertram, one of the young recruits in my company[5]. He had never been in action before and did not like the curious evolutions of the shell which had fallen so close to him. He called out, saying he suddenly felt very ill, and

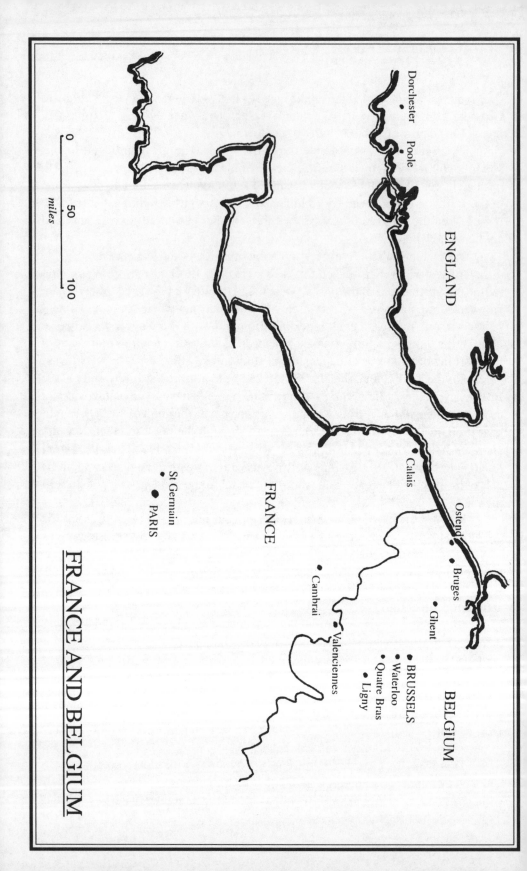

FRANCE AND BELGIUM

had to fall out of rank. I pushed him back.

"Why, Bertram," I said, "it's only the smell of a little bit of powder that's making you sick." But my diagnosis did no good - he fell down and would not go another inch. I was very put out. He ought to have been shot, but I left him.

The right of our line was engaged some time before we were ordered up. By then we had crossed the road and were on the right of a farmhouse called La Haye Sainte. The rain had not quite ceased and the fields and roads were in such a fearfully muddy state, they slowed and tired us. In such conditions it was difficult for the cavalry to perform properly, but they were even worse for the artillery.

About 10 o'clock the action began at Hougoumont on our right, and from there it fell on our centre.

Hougoumont was a walled chateau almost a quarter of a mile in advance of the main British position. It was one of the buildings which Wellington had fortified. Another was the farm at La Haye Sainte. It was at these positions that Napoleon directed his first attacks. Hougoumont was held by the British throughout the action, but La Haye Saint was weaker thereby exposing Wellington's centre, against which Napoleon now concentrated his attack.

Our commanding officer was killed by a musket-shot, but he was soon replaced[6]. We were attacked by a tremendous body of cavalry and infantry and it was only then, owing to the close proximity of the two armies, that the fire from the enemy's cannon - which had been kept up for hours - abated. It was heavy work for us: first we had to form square to receive the attacks of the enemy's cavalry, then form line to meet their infantry. Charge after charge was made on us, but with little success.

British infantry squares consisted of about 500 men, arranged in four ranks. The men in the front rank knelt, the butts of their muskets resting on the ground, the bayonets uppermost and angled outwards. The second rank stood behind them holding their bayonets low. This ring of steel protected the two ranks behind them who, with their rifles levelled at the attacking cavalry, were thus able to pour into the enemy deadly volleys at close-range. The artillery was protected in the centre of the square. Where the guns were positioned in advance of the infantry, the artillerymen fired at the advancing cavalry and then ran back to the safety of the square. The square in which Lawrence fought was one of about 20; they were staggered.

On the turnpike road to the left of us was a brigade of German cavalry with light horses and men. Bonaparte's Bodyguards charged them and wreaked so much havoc that they were routed. Fortunately the Life Guards and Scotch Greys appeared immediately and, after some close handwork, the Bodyguards were compelled to fall back before them. Though many had been cut to pieces, they reformed and came at us again. We threw ourselves into three squares with our artillery in the centre. We were told not to fire at the men, who wore armour, but at their horses. We obeyed and as soon as they got close enough, we opened a deadly fire on them. Very few escaped. They had managed to capture our guns, but fire from our three squares recovered them again. It was almost funny to see these Guards in their chimney-armour trying to run away after their horses had been shot from under them. They made little progress, and many were taken prisoner by those of our light companies who were out skirmishing.

This must have finished Bonaparte's Bodyguards, for we saw no more of them; however, the enemy's infantry started advancing again. We formed line to meet them and again allowed them to get well within musket-shot before firing, then we charged and gave them a good start back again, but not without loss on our side. As soon as they had disappeared, the cavalry - hoping to be amongst us before we could form squares - charged us again, but our persistent fire turned them.

Our numbers became terribly thinned by the successive charges, and by the enemy's cannon during the short intervals in between, yet we did not lose a single inch of ground the whole day. The men were very tired and did begin to despair, but the officers cheered them on: "Keep your ground!" they cried. It's a mystery to me how it was accomplished, for there were scarcely enough of us left to form square[7].

About 4 o'clock I was ordered to the colours. Now I was as used to warfare as anyone, but this was one job I did not like at all. That day alone 14 sergeants, and officers in proportion, had been killed or wounded in the duty and the staff and colours were almost cut to pieces. Nevertheless, I went to work as boldly as I could.

That task will never be blotted from my memory. I am an old man now but I remember it as if it were yesterday. I was with a captain and he was so close to me that his right side was touching my left. Within a quarter of an hour, a cannon-shot came and took his head clean off, spattering me all over with his blood.

A man from his company - Marten was his name - witnessed his end. "There goes my best friend," he commented.

"Never mind," said the lieutenant, quickly stepping forward to take his place: "I will be as good a friend to you as the captain."

"I hope not, sir!" said Marten. The lieutenant had misunderstood for Marten was a notorious character in the regiment on account of the dirtiness of his person. He had been in my company but, because of his poor hygiene, had been transferred to the 5th company where this poor captain had tried, and failed, to reform him by giving him extra duty and suchlike as punishment. For all that, Marten was an excellent soldier in the field[8].

It wasn't long before another cavalry charge took place. We saw it coming. Few as we were, we formed squares to await them. We poured volley after volley into them, doing such fearful execution that they had to retire. But we had been

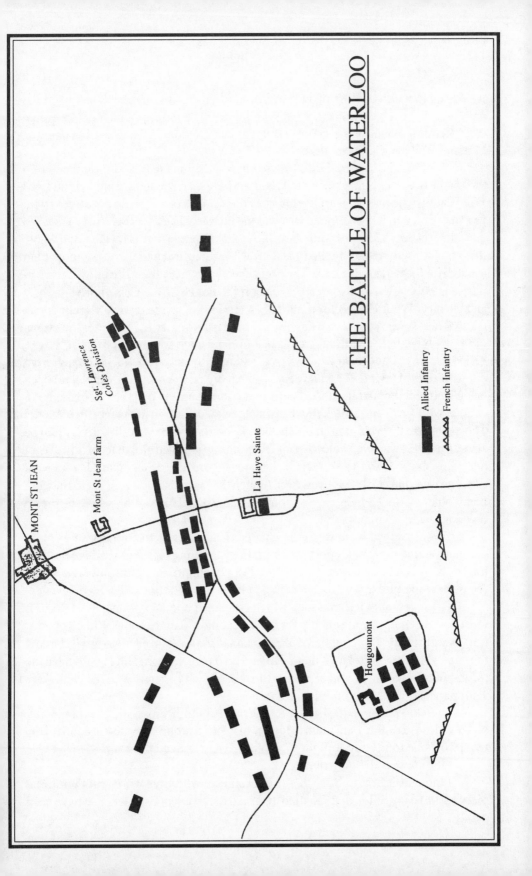

THE BATTLE OF WATERLOO

■ Allied Infantry

△△△△ French Infantry

MONT ST JEAN

Mont St Jean farm

Sgt. Lawrence
Cole's Division

La Haye Sainte

Hougoumont

weakened too with the loss of even more men. We dreaded another charge, but the only help we received was the promise of help. "Keep your ground men," was the cry. "Reinforcements are coming!" But they did not come[9]. The Prussians, under Marshal Blucher, had been detained.

But then, just when the sun started to set, they made their appearance[10]. Up they came in two columns on our left flank and advanced on the enemy's right. Lord Wellington, who had been urging his army on, came to our regiment and asked who was in command. It was Captain Browne and he was given the order to advance. We gave three cheers and set off full of fresh vigour[11]. The attack was made by the whole line and we were joined by the Prussians who were fresh and therefore more than a match for the harassed enemy. The French were forced by their fire into a universal retreat and they fled in disorder, pursued off the field by Blucher's untired infantry and cavalry. We followed for a mile, then encamped on the enemy's ground[12].

There never was a more hungry and tired tribe of men than us after the events of the 18 June, but we still had to make a fire and cook some food. It wasn't easy. Wood was scarce and what there was was sodden. Rouse, one of our company, went out in search of sticks. He came across an enemy powder-wagon which had been taken in the battle and he started cutting the cover up for fuel. His hook came in contact with a nail and struck fire, causing the powder left in the wagon to explode. The explosion threw him high into the air. Remarkably, he was still alive when he came down. He was even able to speak. Everything had been blown from him except one of his shoes. He was a perfect blackguard and in a dangerous state. He said what a fool he was, and cursed his eyes, even though they were both gone. That night, with many other wounded men, he was conveyed to Brussels Hospital, where he died a few days later, raving mad[13].

We succeeded in getting a fire started then, as I was the orderly sergeant to our general that night[14], I reported to him. He was sitting on a gun-carriage holding his horse. When he saw me, he said, "I expect two more sergeants directly, but in the meanwhile please try and get some corn for my poor horse."

Off I went and found a sack which contained about two bushels of corn. It must have been left by the enemy for it was on one of their cannon. When I opened it I was surprised to discover that it also contained a large ham and two fowls. I asked the general if he would accept them. He said he'd take the corn and I could have the meat, but he advised me to keep it out of sight of the Prussians who, he said, were a slippery set of men and might steal it.

I quickly prepared the hanger for the pot by putting cross-sticks over the fire. Not too close - I didn't want them to ignite. Just then a group of these Prussians came by. Two came to my fire to light their pipes. They noticed the ham.

"It looks good," they remarked.

I thought it best to offer them some and so, with my sword, cut them off a piece each. To my relief, that satisfied them and they went off so they must have been on the march, following up the enemy. All that night we could hear the distant sound of cannon and musketry. The ham went into the pot and, when the two other sergeants joined me, the two fowls joined it[15]. In two hours they were pretty well done. It was then I heard someone groaning under a cannon. It was a Frenchman. He was lying on some straw. I thought he was badly wounded and, assuming he was as hungry as me, I went over and told him as best I could that I would bring him some supper when it was cooked, but when I did, he had gone. I wasn't sorry because he left his straw, which made a very good bed for us three sergeants, particularly as the ground was so unpleasantly wet.

We sat down to a good meal of ham and poultry and enjoyed our mess as never before - I had had nothing to eat since early morning. The general did not want us for anything, so we lay on our straw, but I was too tired to sleep. I lay awake a long time, contemplating the scenes of the day. All I had suffered was a scratch on the face, aggravated by the overprimed musket of a private who had been standing next to me. He had been so close that when he fired, the powder had flown up and caught the wound I already had, making me dance without a fiddle for a while.

I don't know how many died that bloody day but the numbers on both sides must have been enormous[16]. In my regiment alone, 300 were missing. The regiment on our right lost 600, mostly as a result of the continual fire kept up by the French cannon in between the charges[17]. Had the Prussians not come up when then did, both armies might have remained on the field of Waterloo, and joined battle again the next day. The French had also been expecting fresh reinforcements but as ours arrived and theirs did not, they had no choice but to retreat.

Next morning we were put in motion in order to prevent our enemy getting a breathing space, but with the Prussians twelve hours in advance of us, we did not have much to fear, unless the French decided to make another stand in their own territory. That might have happened had Blucher not been so close on their heels.

CHAPTER 24

Paris, St Germain, and Matrimony
June 1815 - January 1816

Our march in the direction of Paris was not fatiguing because we halted often and always encamped or were billeted at night[1]. We never encountered the enemy ourselves, but the Prussians collided with them often enough. Our army took some towns, but the march was generally quiet. When we were within a few miles - and in sight of - Paris, we joined up with the Prussians, and halted. The Prussians had opened fire on Paris and it had been returned, but only weakly for the whole city had changed its sentiments away from Napoleon to Louis XVIII, who was with us with about 50 of his guard. They sent out a flag of truce, the firing ceased, terms were agreed, and the city gates were opened[2].

Napoleon Bonaparte was now very unpopular and he fled to the coast hoping to get a ship to America. There were none to hand. Fearing he might be taken prisoner by his own bloodthirsty people, he boarded one of our ships and gave himself up to the captain. The ship was a seventy-four called the *Bellerophon*, commonly know as the 'Billy Ruff'un', so on our march to the city, when thousands of the inhabitants welcomed Louis XVIII with white cockades in their hats and cries of God Save the King, we aggravated them not a little by singing "God save Bonaparte, who has fled and given himself up to the Billy Ruff'uns![3]"

The people wanted to take the horses out of the King's carriage and draw him into the city themselves, but Lord Wellington would not allow it in case, by morning, they had made him shorter by a head! That night, Louis XVIII slept at St Denis, a few miles from Paris. The next morning about 3000 men - with cannon and cavalry - conveyed him into the city. I was with them. A large force was necessary because we were unsure of our welcome. We started at about 11 or 12 o'clock. We met no opposition, the regimental bands struck up, and on we went through streets festooned with flags, with cries of "God save the King!" resounding everywhere. Our destination was the palace where the king was again placed on his throne. He was given a strong guard to protect his person.

We saw no more of Napoleon's army, nor did we want to; most of us had had quite enough of it at Waterloo. Instead we found ourselves comfortably quartered at different barracks throughout the city and here, to ensure that Louis XVIII was thoroughly fixed on his throne, we remained for three months, scarcely wanting for anything but money.

There cannot have been less than 200,000 foreign troops encamped in and around Paris at that time. Two or three times I was one of the king's guards at the palace. What a splendid place it was with fine grounds and a beautiful river running at the back. Nothing else of note occurred apart from the fact that we encamped briefly on Marshal Ney's own property, in front of his residence. In November, Marshal Ney was tried as a traitor by his own country's law, found guilty, and shot[4]. Lord Wellington had nothing to do with it.

But the Bourbons were not popular either. Louis XVIII's heir was assassinated in the streets, but as his duchess had a son soon afterwards there was another member of the family to take his place. Then two men were caught trying to undermine the palace, hoping to blow up the duchess and her child. They were tried and sentenced to be guillotined but the duchess - despite her husband having been killed by the same group - begged their lives of the king, and they were transported for life instead.

While we were in Paris, the whole army was reviewed by two English Dukes, one of whom was the Duke of York[5]. A sham fight was also held where more powder was thrown away than at Waterloo itself! I was every bit as tired afterwards for it lasted all day and we were constantly on the move, whereas at Waterloo we did not advance or retreat more than a 100 yards during the entire action[6].

In Paris, at the rear of our camp, the inhabitants kept up a continual market so we were able to obtain supplies of every description. Sentries guarded it always to prevent plunder. Here, several of the wounded rejoined us from Brussels, and with them was Bertram. As soon as I saw him I put him in the rear-guard as a prisoner and reported him to my captain. Next day a court-martial was held at which I was the chief, but not the only witness against him. As a punishment for absenting himself from the field of action, he was sentenced to 300 lashes. He was tied up and received every lash. This may seem a harsh punishment, but if there had been many like Bertram, the battle of Waterloo would have ended in favour of the French.

He was sent to the hospital for three weeks and when he returned, the captain ordered me to examine his kit. I found his knapsack completely empty, his pouch containing no ammunition. I reported the circumstances to the captain and Bertram was again ordered back to the rear-guard as a prisoner. The next day another court-martial was held on him for making away with his kit, and he was sentenced to another 300 lashes. He received every one without crying out, which was odd because the drummers did not fail in their duty - there was no one they felt more strongly about than a coward. Bertram seemed to have no feeling.

He spent another three weeks in the hospital. Afterwards, the poor fellow was shunned by his comrades. Not only that, he had sixpence a day stopped to pay for his new kit and for the 60 rounds of ball-cartridge which had been supplied to him. As he received only 13 pence a day from which sixpence had been stopped for food, he had only one penny left. Consequently, he was always without money and went missing again, but returned after two or three days. He had been into Paris and sold his kit to maintain himself for those few days. He was again sent to the rear-guard, reported, court-martialled and given another 300 lashes. He went on better for a while but later, when our regiment was in Scotland, he transgressed again and was flogged for a fourth time. When he came out of hospital this time, the colonel ordered his coat to be turned, and a large sheet of paper was pinned on it. It read: "This is a coward, a very bad soldier, and one who had been whipped four times." He was then drummed out of the barracks. I never saw anything of him again, which I was not sorry for; he gave me more trouble than all the rest of my men put together[7].

Towards the end of 1815, the army was moved into winter quarters, chiefly in cantonments[8]. Our brigade went to St Germain, 10 or 12 miles to the north-west of Paris on the River Seine, where we remained for a few months. Outside our barracks was a movable stall which, during the day, was spread out with fruit, spirits, tobacco, snuff, etc. At night, it was cleared away. It was kept by a young woman. Her father was a gardener in business for himself, who used the stall to sell his goods. My first introduction to the woman was when I went to purchase from her a few articles I wanted, but it soon became a usual thing for me to spend most of my spare time at the stall. She gained my affections and for the very first time, I considered marriage.

She had been born Marie Louise Clairet. Bonaparte's first wife was also called Marie Louise and, as he wanted her to be the only one, he issued a proclamation that no-one but the Empress should be called that, so every other Marie-Louise in France had to change their names. Because of Bonaparte's vain freak, Marie Louise Clairet assumed the name of Clotilde[10].

One day, I happened to be at the stall when a soldier of the 27th Regiment, which was also stationed at our barracks, tried to make off with half a pound of tobacco. I pursued and caught him and delivered him to his own regiment, telling them what had happened. I didn't wish to prosecute him so left them to dispose of him as they thought best. I never heard any more. I took the tobacco back to my intended. She was pleased, but what young woman would not have been under the circumstances? Our courtship continued, but only for a short while for, being enamoured of one another, we were anxious to be married.

I explained to my future wife the sort of life she would have to put up with, that at any moment we might have to proceed from her native place, that I might be recalled to England, but she didn't mind.

I made my intentions known to my captain. I knew he would not object. He signed my paper to take to the colonel whose permission I had to get next. The colonel could not understand my marrying a Frenchwoman, but he consented, saying that she would do to teach the soldiers French. He advised me to wait till I got to England but, having got the grant, it was now or never for me. I made arrangements with the army chaplain who fixed the time, and we were duly united.

It cost us nothing. Neither the parson nor clerk looked for any fee, neither were we troubled with any wedding-cake; we simply took ourselves off for a day's merrymaking. I never repented of my decision.

When the order to leave did come, it was at short notice. A farewell had to be taken of her parents whom we never expected to see again. For a time, this cast a slight shadow over my wife's countenance, but it passed in a few days[11].

- CHAPTER 25 -

Cambrai to Glasgow
January 1816 - May 1817

For another year and a half, the 40th Regiment formed part of the army of occupation in France.

From St Germain we marched to Cambrai and were billeted in a nearby village called Aresne[1]. The quarters were very good and the people were kind, as they were in the neighbouring village to which we were shortly moved[2]. But here more unpleasantness took place.

A local farmer who was returning from market was set upon, stripped of everything valuable, and left for dead. His friends, uneasy at his long absence, searched for and found him in a corn field. He was conveyed to his house and attended by a doctor. At the end of a week, he was able to give an account of what happened. He was unsure how much money had been stolen, but said the culprits were two soldiers of the 27th Regiment, who were billeted nearby. An officer was informed and he interviewed the farmer, who said he could recognise the men. As soon as the farmer was able to walk, the officer took him down the ranks of his regiment. Without hesitation, he picked out two men and they had indeed been out at the time of the attack. They were conveyed to the guard-room, and reported to the general. He immediately ordered a court-martial, at which their sergeant said they were often tipsy. They were found guilty, and sentenced to be hanged, which was sanctioned by Lord Wellington.

The men were allowed a week to prepare themselves for their doom, then the brigade was called together to take warning from their unhappy fate. It was a Monday morning. We formed square round the gallows erected for the occasion. In a spring-wagon guarded by a sergeant and twelve men of their regiment, the men were brought under the gallows. A soldier adjusted the ropes and the chaplain read the service. They were asked the question which was usually put in these circumstances. They said they were both guilty and hoped this would be a warning to their comrades. The chaplain then left them, the wagon was moved along, and they were left dancing on nothing.

It did not take long for them to expire but they were left there longer, during which time we had to retain our posts. After an hour they were cut down and each regiment retired solemnly to its own quarters, leaving a company of the men's own regiment to bury them.

It was while the brigade was staying near Cambrai that a captain and five sergeants were selected from each regiment and despatched to Valenciennes, 26 miles away, to learn the sword exercise. From my regiment, Captain Barnard was chosen, and I was one of the five sergeants. There were six hours of sword exercise, six days a weeks for six weeks so we got thoroughly sick of it and were glad to rejoin our regiment.

The regiment had been ordered to go to Leith in Scotland so, the day after our return, we marched to Calais[3]. Every night we were quartered in cantonments, and at one place I met a Jew who gave me 15 francs and a silk dress for a silver watch I had. I changed the French money into English at Calais but was later very put out to discover that, since leaving England, the coinage had changed and I had gained nothing.

We were in Calais for two nights and my wife and I had very comfortable quarters. She had borne the marches as well as me; better sometimes. Three colliers had been contracted to convey our regiment from Calais to Scotland and they were the rickettiest old watertubs I had ever seen! I doubted they would get us there if the weather turned bad[4].

With a fair wind, it was only a three day sail from Calais to Leith, but we had a foul one nearly all the way so the voyage took us seven weeks![5] My wife, who had never seen the sea, found the voyage long and tedious, and was ill at first but, after my American trips, I was used to it, having learned long since not to be troubled by trifles.

At Bridlington in Yorkshire we had to put in and wait for a fair wind, which was three weeks in coming. The first night the major invited the officers to dine with him and sent a quart of beer on board for each man, and half that quantity for each woman. During the day we were allowed to go on shore, but we had to be back on board by 9 o'clock at night.

The inhabitants of Bridlington were kind and offered our women their houses to wash clothes in. Many accepted. It was in Bridlington that I got rid of the silk dress. I had been trying to dispose of almost since I obtained it for, with all the travelling about, my wife did not require it. I used to visit a public-house and the landlord's daughter was a fine-looking girl. She sported a silk dress of her own, but I sold her mine for 50 shillings and a gallon of beer. The beer I gave to her customers.

When a favourable breeze at last sprang up, we set sail again. It took us a whole day to draw near to Shields and a pilot was signalled for, but before he arrived we had to return to Bridlington, which took another 9 hours during which time the vessel rolled so fearfully that the women especially began to despair.

Our second stay in Bridlington lasted ten days. When we got to Shields, we were there a week. Again, we were allowed to go on shore when our walks sometimes extended to the coal-mines. We also went over the glass-manufactories, which really amused my wife. In order for us to see the process, the workmen made her a smelling-bottle and me several pipes and a walking-stick, out of glass.

From Shields we went on to Leith and landed[6]. All our baggage was examined at the customs house, so it was a good thing I had managed to sell that silk dress! We stayed the night in Leith and marched towards Glasgow the next day, reaching it on the third day.

CHAPTER 26

Family Reunion
May - December 1817

The barracks at Glasgow were comfortable. We were there three months when the winter of 1817 set in. Furloughs were granted for two months to a part of the regiment. As I had a wife with me, and as my home was so far away, I gave my furlough to a fellow-sergeant so that he might go to Ireland, but I wrote home and told them I had arrived in Scotland. I received a reply from my mother saying my father was ill and that if I did not come and see him then, I might never see him again.

I consulted my wife and, as she readily consented to come with me, I took the old lady's letter to the captain to try for another furlough.

"There are so many gone, sergeant, that I don't know whether the colonel will let you," he said, "but we'll ask him."

We went to the colonel and when he learned the nature of my case, he agreed to allow me six weeks. He signed my furlough and advanced me one shilling per day for the time I would be away. I had lately received my Waterloo prize-money of £20, but had already made a few purchases, like clothing and a watch, the sort of things that make one feel a little more respectable.

I planned to sail from Leith to London and then walk to Briantspuddle.[1] We reached Leith after a two day march. Next morning I booked a passage for two on a Leith trader bound for London. The captain charged 2½ guineas, including board. We sailed - on time - the following day but, owing to a heavy wind, were obliged to run in to Berwick and anchor. There a revenue cutter, which was cruising too close, knocked the bowsprit off our little vessel disabling her for three days. When all was put right we again set sail. We had a fair wind and a speedy journey. Arriving in the London Docks at night we remained on board till the following morning.

After breakfast, we started for Piccadilly, which we found only after a good deal of inquiry. A hackney cab drove up and the driver asked where we were going. We told him and he said he would put us into the right road for 2 shillings. I offered him 18 pence, but he would not take us for that, so we got him to show us the way and started walking. We had got no farther than Hyde Park Corner when the same cab overtook us and stopped again. The driver said he thought he could take us for the money now. He was a sharp fellow looking for a double fair. He already had a passenger - a gentlemen - whom he asked if we could join him as we were going in the same direction. The man politely consented so we were forked in by cabby, who shot off as if the whole road was his own.

I spoke French to my wife because she did not understand English and I mentioned this to the gentleman. He said he knew a little French himself. He noticed the medal on my breast.

"I see you were at the battle of Waterloo, sergeant?"

"Yes," I replied, "and many others besides."

So the conversation began and we soon became friendly. He wanted to know where I was bound. I told him and he kindly asked me to spend a week at his house on the way, saying I should not want for anything. I declined, explaining the reason for my hurry, but thanked him for his kindness. At this point his stage expired and he got out, but he first insisted on giving my wife 5 shillings and paying our fare. He wished us good-speed on our journey and we shook hands heartily and parted.

After alighting from the cab ourselves, we walked some distance to a village where the Salisbury road-wagon put up. Being hungry we entered a public-house and had some tea. At nightfall, I was enjoying myself over my tobacco when in came ten or twelve people. I decided to amuse them by spinning a yarn. I made them shake with laughter, but what tickled them most was to hear me and my wife speak French. She was annoyed because she did not know what they were laughing at.

We were still there at 10 o'clock when the party broke up. I called for my bill. To my surprise I found that as well as the fourpence for a glass of gin for myself, the landlady had charged 8 pence for the boiling water! As we had found our own food, tea, and sugar, I asked her if it was a mistake? She said it wasn't. I paid her but said I wished she and her charges were on the other side of the moon, and that, if we had been in France, we would have got our boiled water for nothing!

The road-wagon was due to start for Salisbury at midnight and the wagoner agreed to take us for two shillings. He said we could get in straight away, which we did. We were so tired, we lay down and fell fast asleep. When we awoke, we found ourselves jogging along and arrived in Salisbury late the next night. We remained in Salisbury for the rest of the night and made an early start the next morning. We marched 7 miles, had breakfast, then did not halt again till we got to Blandford, where we stayed the night.

The next morning was Sunday and we travelled the 8 miles from Blandford to my native village, arriving during the morning church service. We took a short cut through the churchyard and went up the village, inquiring at several houses where John Lawrence - my father - lived. That way, I learned not only that he still lived in the house in which I was born, but that he was much better.

I was now in no hurry to get home so I strolled into a house owned by a woman I had known well before I left. She was old now. I asked her where John Lawrence lived as I had seen his son who had given me a message for him. But the woman's piercing eyes were not so easily deceived: She recognized me as a Lawrence, but did know whether I was William or John. I told her I was William and she immediately ran off to bring my sister.

As you can imagine, the appearance of two strangers entering so many houses in this country place had set it astir, particularly as one was dressed as a soldier. Now that they knew who we were, it was telegraphed all through the village. I set off for home, but before I could get to my own door my sister was upon me, trying to kiss me[2]. I had not shaved since I left Scotland so my long thick beard and moustache made it almost a fruitless task.

"Come in!" she cried out. "Why don't you shave?"

There was no barber handy so she said she would shave me as she always shaved father, so in I went. My wife could hardly make sense of what was going on but seemed reluctant to interrupt with a word of French to me; and it had not yet occurred to my sister to ask me who this mysterious woman was! My wife followed me indoors without any questioning and, like myself, sat down. I pulled off my knapsack.

My father and mother were still at church. The shaving-tackle was brought out, and my sister started on me, but it so put me in mind of the ceremony of Crossing the Line that I became impatient, opened my knapsack, took out my own razor, and finished the job myself.

By this time church was over. I put my head out of the door, and there was my brother.[3] When he saw me, he could scarcely speak. He was alone - my father and mother had stopped to take the sacrament. The old lady though must have got scent of something for when I did see her, she was coming along like a spread-eagle in the same old black bonnet and red cloak that she had worn when I left. I went to meet her. She was so overcome with emotion at my sudden reappearance that I had to lean her up against the house to prevent her falling. The old man was coming along behind, quite infirm, and hobbling on two sticks. I went to him next and he behaved worse than any of them! I led him in and, with some difficulty, got him to a chair. For a long time neither one of us spoke.

"My child," he said at last, "I did not expect to see you again." It had been twelve years since I had left them at Dorchester.

My wife, without understanding a word, was much affected by this scene. I threw a word or two of explanation to her in French, which surprised them all a good deal! They were no less astonished when I told them she was my wife. It must have been queer for her to be in a foreign land with these strangers around her, but by the evening we were all reconciled to one another. Dozens of friends and neighbours came in to see us. My wife, knowing they could not all be relations, wanted to know what they wanted. I told her they had come to see her as they had never seen a Frenchwoman before, but she would not believe this flattery.

I decided we ought to wet the subject a little, but there was no public-house in the village. The nearest was three miles off at Puddletown[4], so I got one of my brothers to go there. He brought back four gallons and we made ourselves comfortable till 10 o'clock when we went to bed - in the same room I had slept in all those years ago.

After a good night's rest we rose early. Everyone had recovered, except the old lady, who still had not done piping. After breakfast I took a walk round the village and met the clergyman[5]. He insisted on taking me to his house and giving me some ale. He kept me there for at least an hour, talking about the war and the religion of the countries I had been in. I was glad to get away, but then I had to spend the rest of the day visiting other people in the village. The next day was even worse for my mother brought out every single letter I had sent and made me listen to them being read out. By the evening I was almost crazy! I advised her to burn the lot.

"Never, William," she said, "not as long as I live," and she put them back in their place.[6]

We passed the next two days visiting those of my brothers and sisters who lived nearby[7]. I could not rest in one place for long so, on the third morning, I set out with my wife to see another brother who was a farm-labourer in Corfe Mullen, about twelve miles of. After some enquiries for George Lawrence, I found his house. The door was answered by his wife who I had know before her marriage, but she did not know who I was[8]. I asked for George. She pointed to the barn and I went over. He was there, threshing.

"Hello friend, do you thresh by the day or the quarter?" I asked him.

"By the quarter," he answered, "but I cannot do much of it."

He stared at me but he did not know me for I had on my regimentals.

"Is there a public-house handy?" I asked him.

"There's one just below."

"That must be hard work. Come with me to the public house and I'll treat you."

He thanked me and led the way.

I ordered some beer, and tobacco with pipes, then I took off my shako[9]. He recognised me immediately! He took me back to his home to meet his wife and we stayed with him for two days. We returned to Briantspuddle and remained with the old people for the rest of the 18 days I had allotted for our stay (the journey to and from Briantspuddle accounting for the rest of my leave).

The morning we left was just as bad as the morning we arrived. My wife, who had got used to the old people, was as loud as any of them. At last, being sick of the whole affair, I buckled on my knapsack, bid them good-bye and took myself off, leaving my wife to follow with my brother, who had volunteered to go with us as far as Dorchester.

I planned a different route for our journey back, intending to find at Bristol a ship to take us to Scotland so, when we parted from my brother, we went westwards. Our first night's stop was at a roadside public-house just outside Dorchester. Our route next morning took us through Sherborne. On the way to

Bristol we met Warren, a member of the light company of my regiment. He was on his way to London to get a ship back to Scotland. I told him our route and he said he would like to accompany us, that he had no money, and would I lend him some? I said no as I had very little myself, but I said that if he came with us, and lived as we did, I would pay for his food and lodging till we got to the regiment. He agreed. When we got to Bristol there was no ship going to Scotland so my wife, who was an excellent walker, proposed going all the way by road so, the following day, we set off. We usually did two stages a day, and our route took us through Gloucester, Worcester, Manchester, Carlisle, and so to Glasgow. It was a long and tedious march. Our companion, who was anything but pleasant, left us at Manchester.

We got back to barracks in Glasgow one day before my furlough expired. All I had in my pocket was twopence-halfpenny, having sold my watch for subsistence on the way. I reported, and drew my remaining 10 pence a day for the six weeks, although a penny a day was deducted for small beer, which wasn't allowed while I was away. My wife had been frostbitten during the march and soon after our arrival at the barracks, she became very ill, remaining so for more than a week.

- CHAPTER 27 -

Veteran and Farm Labourer
January 1818 - July 1821

While in Glasgow, General Sir George Osborne, the head colonel of our regiment, came expressly to review us. He was an old man and had not seen the regiment for years. After going through our facings, we were arranged in a square, into which the old gentleman entered to present us with a new stand of colours. He addressed us for what he said was the last time and said he hoped his colours would endure as well as the old, and be crowned with an equal amount of victory. On them The Peninsula and Waterloo were engraved in gilt letters. He then took his farewell leave and each man received sixpence from him to drink his health.

Soon afterwards the army was reduced and our regiment was cut from a 1000 strong to 600[1]. The old and disabled were discharged first, then lots were cast to make up the remainder. Amongst the sergeants, the lot fell on me so, a month later, I and nine others were ordered to Chatham.

We marched to Leith, embarked on the Leith packet and, after some very rough weather, landed at Gravesend. We moved on to Chatham where we remained for six weeks waiting to pass the board. We re-embarked on a small craft at Gravesend and went up river to the Tower of London. From there we marched to Chelsea Hospital.

The next morning, we were examined by the doctor, and then called up before the board, one at a time. When it was my turn, I was asked my age and length of service. One of the gentlemen called out "Seven!" but the doctor immediately said "Nine!" because of the wound in my knee. This meant I should receive a pension of ninepence a day for that was what was settled on me for life. I went to an office, where I received my expenses to Dorchester - one shilling and tenpence for myself, and three-halfpence for my wife, for every ten miles. With that we set off for Briantspuddle again, walking every step of the way[2].

When my wife and I arrived in Briantspuddle everyone was well. I did not want to stay there long so, on the following morning, we took our leave and we went to Studland where I had been apprenticed, and which I therefore claimed rightly as my parish[3].

We put up at a public-house until I could procure a house and some furniture, which took me about a week. My wife and I could hardly live on a pension of ninepence a day so my next task was to find work. I soon obtained employment on a farm close by for a wage of ten shillings a week. I was only a labourer, and the work came very hard at first, but I soon got used to it. For nine months I worked for this master, a former captain in the navy who was sharp, but just. I left because I received a sudden call to rejoin the army.

I was ordered to Plymouth, setting out on 5 November 1819. In Plymouth I joined the 3rd Veteran Battalion, which was about a 1000 strong and from there we sailed to Ireland. We landed at the Cove of Cork and marched through Cork to Fermoy. From Fermoy it took us two or three days to get to Templemore. We were there about a month when three companies of the regiment, myself included, were ordered to Tralee in County Kerry. On our arrival, a detachment consisting of a lieutenant, a sergeant (myself), a corporal, and 17 men, were sent to Dingle, situated on a large tongue of land[4]. There we were stationed in barracks for about a year[5], our principal duty being to guard the coast in order to prevent smuggling. We were under the command of a coastguard captain called Collis.

Smuggling was prevalent at that time and the manoeuvres of the inhabitants, who were practised in this art, astonished me. Once, information was received that a certain house contained smuggled tobacco so the captain called me out. With 11 men, we went to search it. At the door we were met by three ruffianly-looking Irishmen, whose conversation we could not understand at all, but we went in anyway. At one end three cows were standing. We searched the house but found nothing. We were about to search outside, when I noticed that the three men were laughing. Suspicious now, I turned the cows out and looked under the litter where I discovered a trap-door. I opened it. A flight of steps led down into a cellar in which were at least twenty bales of tobacco. We brought it up, but still not content, we searched the garden as well. The ground had recently been disturbed so we disturbed it again and discovered twelve more bales concealed there. All the tobacco was conveyed in press-carts to the captain's house. For our services, we received a good supper and extra pay. Mine amounted to half a crown. The privates received less.

Another time when we were out we passed a funeral. We presented arms and only found out afterwards that under the pall had been a coffin-shaped box containing nothing but smuggled tobacco! That was how it was being conveyed.

These, and similar incidents, were frequent during our stay, for the local inhabitants were of the wildest sort. Once a cotton-ship was driven ashore and we had the greatest difficulty preventing them from plundering it.

We were eventually ordered back to Plymouth. Rejoining our companions at Tralee we marched to Waterford Harbour and embarked on our transport, arriving at Plymouth in about June 1821[6]. This marked the end of my military career. It had lasted 17 years and 7 months[7], most of which was spent on active service. During my stay with the 3rd Veteran Battalion, my pension had been stopped, but I was discharged on the same pension as before.

From Plymouth I and my wife marched back to Studland. We took a house

and my master immediately took me back to work. However, I drifted about
between one or two trades[8]. Finally I took a little public-house and my wife and I
lived pretty prosperously till she died. Feeling unwell myself, I thought it best to
give up the public-house and stop working[9]. I wrote to the authorities at Chelsea and,
through the influence of a kind gentleman, I obtained an additional threepence a day
on my pension, making a shilling in all. I am now living in a house which has been
bequeathed to me by my late master for as long as I live[10] and am as comfortable
as these circumstances, and the interposition of a few friends can make me.

To conclude, I will say that I have striven as well as my imperfect faculties
will allow, and in such a way that it can be read in a few hours, to sum up the main
scenes of my life, and the various campaigns in which I served. I am sorry I cannot
give the reader fuller details of the Peninsula and Waterloo, but I am sure that if any
of my comrades were to take up this work and examine it, they would say that such
information as I have been able to give, is accurate.

- EPILOGUE -

Why did William Lawrence decide to tell his story? Was it at the urging of friends and neighbours as George Nugent Bankes said in the Preface to the 1886 edition of the autobiography, or was it simply because he wanted to?

By the 1850s, several eyewitness accounts of the military campaigns in which Lawrence had fought had been published, notably *Reflections of a Rifleman* by Harris (1829), and *Adventures in the Rifle Brigade* by Kincaid (1830). Although unable to read them himself, Lawrence may have been aware of their existence. At a time when old age had reduced his earning power, did it occur to him that the tale of his military exploits might have a commercial value?

Lawrence, acknowledging that his memoirs might be read by former comrades, strove for accuracy, but he did exercise a degree of self-censorship. His restraint in recounting atrocities committed during the Peninsular War is commendable, and the subtle inaccuracies surrounding both his status as a charity apprentice, and the timing of his marriage, understandable. What is less admirable is that, after informing his readers that his aim was to sum up the 'leading scenes' of his life, he then leaves out almost everything after 1821!

The 1820s and 1830s were a time of great hardship for the poor in Dorset. Social injustice created civil unrest, yet of this, and of its effect on him and his family, Lawrence says nothing. Was his civilian life really so uneventful? Or is the truncated nature of his autobiography yet another example of his prudence? With the help of archive material held at the County Record Office in Dorchester, it is possible to cast some light into this shady area of his life, so we'll begin in 1819, in his home parish of Affpuddle, to which he was despatched on his discharge from the 40th Regiment.

Once he had got used to it, life in the army suited William. Given a choice, he would probably have remained a soldier, so the prospect of returning to civilian life as a farm labourer in Affpuddle may have been unwelcome to him, particularly as the local magistrate was still James Frampton (1769-1855), from whose jurisdiction he had escaped in 1805 by enlisting in the army. Frampton, who was also the local squire, was not a presence to be ignored so what was his attitude towards William Lawrence going to be? Would the young man be welcomed back into the local community as a hero of Waterloo, or be remembered as a rogue?

James Frampton's view of William Lawrence - if he had one - is not recorded, but his repressive instincts towards those who challenged his authority is well-documented. Evidence of it exists in the correspondence of the Frampton Education Foundation, a charity of which he was a trustee. The FEF had been set up to place the children of the poor from the parishes of Moreton, Affpuddle and Turnerspuddle in apprenticeships. This arrangement was less philanthropic than it sounds because it could be used as a convenient way of exporting pauper children to other parishes, where they became little more than unpaid drudges. William Lawrence had been one of the FEF's apprentices and although no correspondence about his experience has survived, he wasn't Henry Bush's only apprentice...

In April 1803, a year before William, the FEF had sent Bush an Affpuddle youth called Thomas Linnington. Four years later - two years after William had run away - Bush complained to the charity about Linnington's behaviour. The exchange of letters has survived. They are so revealing that they are worth quoting in full. The earliest is from Reverend John Morton Colson, Rector of Studland, and himself a magistrate. It is addressed to James Frampton. The letter it refers to no longer exists.

Corfe Castle, Feb 28 1807

> Sir, I was desired a few days since by my parishioner Henry Bush, to read your letter to his apprentice Thomas Linnington and, if possible, add to the good advice it contained. I must say Linnington heard me with the most inattentive and impertinent countenance I ever beheld, acknowledged the charges of being out late - once during the whole night - to be true, but did not consider them as offences and, in my presence, recriminated against his Master in very insolent and daring language, in consequence of which I granted a summons for him to appear at Wareham on the 8 March, and take the liberty of troubling you with this, thinking you might wish some person from the Parish of Moreton to attend.

The reply, from James Frampton, on 6 March 1807 was this:

> Sir, I feel much obliged by your kind attention in acquainting me with the misbehaviour of Thos. Linnington and of your having in consequence been obliged to summons him to appear before you to answer the complaint of this Master Henry Bush. I cannot have the smallest wish to have any person attend on the part of the Trustees, being perfectly satisfied that ample justice will be done between the parties. I will only trouble you by requesting you will have the goodness to inform the boy that, by his misconduct, he has already forfeited all claim to any allowance of monies at the expiration of his apprenticeship towards assisting him in setting up his trade, as that is never granted by the Trustees but as a reward for uninterrupted good behaviour.

Whatever the basis was of the legal system in Dorset in the early 1800s, it had nothing to do with justice, 'ample' or otherwise. On this evidence its primary purpose was to ensure that the arbitrary judgements of landowner-philanthropists were given the force of law.

Regrettably, Colson's instant bias against Linnington has censored the young man's 'recriminations' against Henry Bush so we don't know what they were, but neither did Frampton so why did he show no inclination to find out? Why instead did he abandon the youth, for whose welfare the charity had taken responsibility, by denying him representation in court? Frampton's concern for the boy's welfare is negligible. Interested only in maintaining the hierarchy of power, he prejudged the outcome of the court hearing and penalised Linnington by withdrawing from him not only his reward for having put up with Henry Bush for four years, but one of his few incentives for submitting himself to more of the same for another three years. Neither Frampton nor Colson question Bush's motive, or appear suspicious of his lack of success with apprentices. Were they naive? Were they so used to imposing simple solutions on complex situations that they never developed an ability to understand them?

The final letter explains how the situation was resolved. It was sent by James Frampton on 19 February 1811 to Alexander Clarke of Gosport, in reply to an enquiry from Mr Clarke.

> Sir, I wish it was in my power to accede to your request respecting Thomas Linnington's Indentures, particularly as I hope he may have become more steady since his marriage with a person who deserves encouragement from her long service in your family. I am extremely sorry that Linnington should find difficulty in obtaining employment, but since the receipt of your letter I have consulted some others of the Trustees of the Charity by which he was apprenticed, and we are all of (the) opinion that it would be unfair to any Master who wishes to employ him if we sent him his Indentures, as it would give them reason to suppose that he had served out his time in a proper manner when in fact he did not serve for above four years of the time for which he was apprenticed, and during that time his conduct was so irregular, and his behaviour to his Master so improper, that Mr Bush (his master) was obliged to lay a complaint against him before a Magistrate, in whose presence Linnington also conducted himself with great insolence.
>
> Mr Bush being at that time in a very bad state of health was not able to keep this wild young man under control, nor at last to find him in sufficient work, in consequence of which the Trustees, at the request of both parties, consented that the Indentures should be

cancelled which was done accordingly.

Under these circumstances we feel that we should not be justified in sending Linnington his Indentures although we are anxious that he should be able to get an honest livelihood and recover the injury he has done himself by his irregular behaviour in his youth.

Having read this, is it surprising that William Lawrence chose to run away from Henry Bush rather than complain to anyone in authority about his behaviour? Young as he was, William seems to have appreciated that James Frampton was the greater threat to him. In 1819, when he returned to Briantspuddle, was Frampton still a threat? Is that why, within 24 hours of arriving, William left Affpuddle Parish to start a new life elsewhere?

William and Clotilde went to the Purbeck coast, but why Studland? Lawrence knew the hamlet and says that, as it was the place he had been apprenticed, he claimed it 'rightly as my parish', but how strong was that claim? For a start, the FEF records describe Henry Bush as being a 'builder and stonemason' of *Swanage* Parish, although it is obvious from the involvement of the Rev John Morton Colson, Rector of Studland, in the correspondence concerning Linnington, that Bush's connections with Studland were equally strong. A poor youth could qualify for settlement rights in a parish by being apprenticed there for seven years, but a broken apprenticeship *did not count*. William's claim was invalid and he knew it, but that did not stop him going to Studland and, despite having been a runaway apprentice, he was allowed to stay. How did he get away with it?

His Waterloo medal must have helped. Having been at the battle which finally destroyed the power of Napoleon, William would have been regarded as a hero, and might have received special consideration, but there was probably a more practical reason for his acceptance - his army pension. Granted to him for life, it would have reassured the churchwardens and overseers of Studland that he would never become a burden on parish funds. And being childless was a boon. If William and Clotilde had had dependent children, they would not have found it so easy to reject his home parish and gamble on acceptance in another. But was it a gamble? It is worth considering whether Lawrence had other connections with the parish.

In 1819 the owner of Studland was Henry Bankes (1757-1834). In 1813, during the Peninsular War, Henry's son and heir, William John (1786-1855), went to Spain and was, for a short while, attached to Wellington's headquarters. William John was not a soldier but a traveller and art collector. The Peninsular War had displaced a large number of the paintings once housed in Spanish convents and cathedrals, and Bankes acquired some of them. He sent them back to the family home of Kingston Lacy, near Wimborne in Dorset, where they hang today. One is a fragment from an altarpiece by Murillo which is reputed to have been discovered in the knapsack of a French soldier who had been killed. The question we have to ask is this: while in Spain, did William John Bankes have any contact with the Spanish-speaking Corporal Lawrence? If Lawrence had been of service to Bankes and therefore knew of the Bankes family's ownership of Studland, would that have given him the confidence to apply for settlement status in 1819?

It is an interesting theory but there is not a shred of evidence to prove that William Lawrence and William John Bankes ever met in England, let alone in Spain, so we are left with excuses for his decision to live in Studland, not a satisfactory reason.

So what was it about the isolated hamlet, adjoining a softly shelving beach, that attracted this young, restless, French-speaking ex-soldier? What was it about the sheltered bay, about Ballard Down with its rugged cliffs and waterline caves, that appealed to this cunning ex-plunderer whose father-in-law in France was a peddlar of spirits and tobacco? Was it the prospect of working long hours as a labourer on a Studland farm for ten shillings a week, or was it the prospect of earning much larger sums in less regular employment? In his nine months as an apprentice, had William Lawrence learned that Studland was a smuggler's paradise?

At the Public Record Office in Kew is a copy of a report sent from the Poole Customs House to the Board in London. It informs them that, in 1804 (the year of Lawrence's apprenticeship), no less than 40,000 gallons of spirit were landed illegally on the coast of Purbeck, carried inland and hidden 'in caves and other secret places', before being transported to retailers in Bath, Bristol, Trowbridge and other manufacturing towns. The key landing sites were South Haven Point, Durlston, Seacombe, Dancing Ledge, Winspit, Freshwater, Kimmeridge, and *Studland Bay*.

Contraband alcohol was usually conveyed in tubs, each holding about four gallons each, so the 40,000 gallons had probably been 'spirited' away from the Purbeck coast in about 10,000 tubs, a labour intensive task, as another Customs report demonstrates:

In September 1824, the crew of the Swanage preventive boat was on duty near the coast when they encountered a group or 20 or 30 men carrying tubs. Two men were caught, but the rest escaped by running off in different directions still carrying their booty. The usual way for a man to carry tubs was in pairs in a harness over his shoulders, so the absconding smugglers may have accounted for about 50 tubs. As another 42 were discovered nearby in an abandoned cart, the total consignment must have been about 100 tubs. If 20 or 30 men were need to shift 100 tubs then it gives you some idea of how much labour would have been needed to shift 10,000. That manpower was supplied locally. There was no shortage because a labourer could earn more money in one night carrying tubs for the local smugglers than he could in a whole week on a farm. The gentry tolerated the trade either because they were funding the smuggling runs themselves, or because the supplementary income it afforded the men took pressure off them to raise the low wages which had tempted their workforce into criminal activity in the first place.

It is interesting to speculate whether the friction between Henry Bush and his two young apprentices may have been caused by smuggling? Think about it. Wouldn't carrying tubs for smugglers have afforded a sturdy apprentice a chance to earn money which he could earn no other way? And wouldn't that income have reduced his master's absolute power over him?

There is no doubt that apprentices did become involved. In December 1832, John Webber who was 15 and then residing in Broadmayne, was killed on the beach at Weymouth. The entry in the Register for his home parish of Sydling St Nicholas reads:

This boy was shot by coastguards having been employed by his master, a glazier, to assist smugglers to carry away their tubs.

But what if the apprentice was involved in a smuggling operation from which his master was excluded? Do you recall the misdemeanour which earned William Lawrence a thrashing from Henry Bush? It was being out late. And what made Henry Bush complain to James Frampton about Thomas Linnington? He had been out late too, 'once *during the whole night*'. On that night, had Linnington been carrying tubs for the local smugglers? And is that how young William Lawrence developed a taste for the small beer which only money could buy? And in deciding to return to Studland, was it William Lawrence's intention to supplement his army pension - and satisfy his sense of adventure - by engaging in smuggling?

We don't know because of the paucity of evidence. Smuggling was a shady occupation in which the participants were bound together, not by written contracts, but by ties of loyalty similar to those among serving soldiers. The names of some of those who were involved are documented, but only because they got caught! 'William Lawrence' was not one of them.

What does Lawrence himself say about the period between 1821 and 1844? He implies that he was not a farm labourer for long, but 'drifted about between one of two trades'. Was 'free-trading' one of them? If not, then how was he was making a living? In the Census of 1841, Lawrence and Clotilde are not listed as having an occupation; William declared himself to be an army pensioner, and Clotilde was 'independent'. William said himself that he could not live on his pension, so how was he subsidising their self-proclaimed independence?

It is very difficult to say because his name does not appear in Bankes Estate documents until 1836 when he is recorded as having been paid on a regular basis to look after the Studland plantations, to plant trees and repair fences. His remuneration never came to more than £4 a year, which was about a third of the annual value of his pension, and a fifth of what he could have earned as a farm labourer, so how was he making up the shortfall? He did not have the temperament to be a farmer, nor the inclination to be a farm labourer. What he did have was the guile, the experience, the contacts, and perhaps the freedom, to operate successfully as a smuggler. Perhaps all he needed to put them into practice was the incentive?

For 18 months, William was in Ireland with the Third Veteran Battalion. His task? To combat Irish smugglers. He proved a wily opponent and earned a small bonus for detecting a large hoard of contraband, but he knew very well that a smuggler could earn much, much more from a large hoard of undetected contraband, so did this 'gamekeeper' turn 'poacher'?

Remember how, during the Torres Vedras campaign in Portugal, the Major in the 40th Regiment had tried to tempt Lawrence and his comrades to reveal the whereabouts of the hoard of gold dollars they had found in the cellar? He failed because, underestimating the venality of the men, his bribe fell far short of what each of them had stolen.

Lawrence had a code of honour of sorts, but it did not stretch to doing himself out of ill-gotten gains he stood every chance of holding on to, nor did it include incriminating himself. He was a keen judge of what was in his best interests. He was happy to tell his readers about acts of plunder during the Peninsular War because he knew no-one was going to call him to account for what had been done in a foreign country 50 years earlier, but it would have been dangerous for an unconvicted smuggler to recall his feats of derring-do in cheating the Crown out of its customs revenue, perhaps as little as 10 years before. If Lawrence was a smuggler then, like Jack Rattenbury of Beer in Devon, his 'career' may have spanned more than 30 years. He would not have been the first publican to peddle contraband goods - Tom Lucas, landlord of the Ship Inn at Wool, was at it in 1827. However, as the evidence is circumstantial, you will have to make up your own minds about whether or not William Lawrence was a smuggler.

In editing out of his autobiography nearly 40 years of his life, William also edited out his family, yet a close study of archive documents relating to Studland reveals that, from about 1832 to 1856, Henry Lawrence, William's eldest brother, was also his neighbour.

In 1799, when he was 15, Henry Lawrence was apprenticed by James Frampton's charity to blacksmith John Alder of Bere Regis. This is of interest because, during that time, Alder became one of the chief actors in an incident of 'witchcraft' documented in the diary of Reverend William Ettricke, Vicar of Affpuddle and Rector of Turnerspuddle from 1787 to 1808. The story is worth telling here not only because of the Affpuddle-Frampton-Lawrence connection - it happened in 1804, the year of William's apprenticeship - but because it is another example of the ignorance in which even educated men of the time wallowed:

In February 1804, hearing that she was both good and cheap, Ettricke employed Susan Woodrowe, a local woman, as his gardener. At first he was pleased

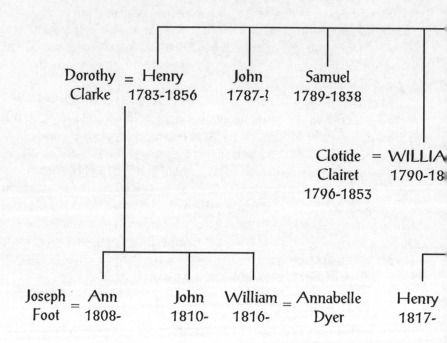

The Lawrence Family

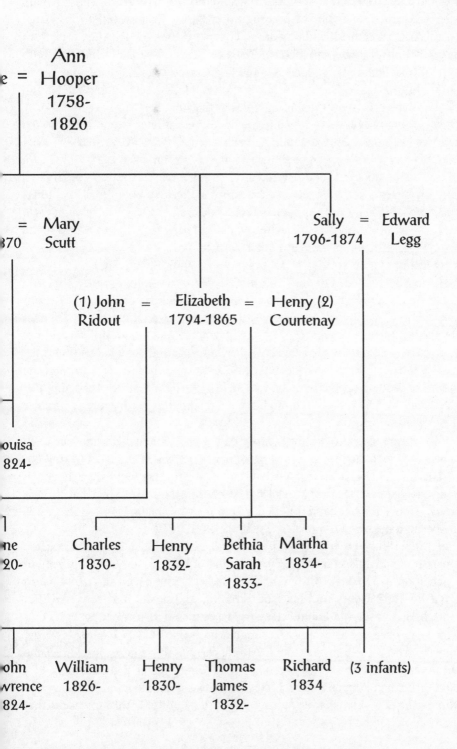

Ann
e = Hooper
1758-
1826

= Mary
370 Scutt

Sally = Edward
1796-1874 Legg

(1) John = Elizabeth = Henry (2)
Ridout   1794-1865   Courtenay

ouisa
824-

ne   Charles   Henry   Bethia   Martha
20-   1830-   1832-   Sarah   1834-
                           1833-

ohn   William   Henry   Thomas   Richard   (3 infants)
vrence   1826-   1830-   James   1834
824-   1832-

with her and praised her work. Some days later, his horse fell ill. He diagnosed a pain in the bowels which he treated by pouring a drench of gin and warm ale down the animal's throat. The remedy didn't work so he sent for John Alder. Alder took from the horse a couple of quarts of blood before putting down 2 balls of soap, and 'reub and nitre of the vicar's own preparing'. The horse saw sense and recovered, but in September fell ill again. Back comes John Alder, bleeds it again and feeds it an ointment which so blisters the animal's throat that that has to be treated too. A drench, a cooling purge, and a rowel in the horse's chest later, Alder is dismissed by the formidable Mrs Ettricke and another farrier, Charles Way, sent for. Way laughs derisively at old Alder's methods and poisonous remedies and rubs his own concoction on the horse's throat. He and the vicar redouble their efforts on the sick animal with such success that, on 14 September, it dies. By now, Ettricke's grass seed has failed, his baby son has been unwell, a sick pig has had to be slaughtered, and the horse he borrowed to replace his own is suffering from - yes - a pain in the bowels. All these miseries were too much for Ettricke so, in November, he pays Alder for killing the horse, and sacks Susan Woodrowe for causing it!

Having decided that his misfortunes are due to nothing less than the 'vile witchcraft of a bad neighbour', Susan Woodrowe, his once cheap and cheerful gardener, is now insidiously labelled an 'ill-tempered' wretch with a 'malignant grin' by the learned clergyman. The distraught woman, ignorant of the cause of her fall from grace, writes letters to Ettricke in an attempt to find out what she has done wrong, and to try to get her job back, but Ettricke threatens her with a warrant if she persists. "She thought proper to obey," wrote Ettricke, "for fear of Mr Frampton, who does not like her, and only through my interceding for her forbore to turn her out of her possessions."

Poor Susan Woodrowe, thrown out of her job without warning and then threatened with legal action, and the loss of her home, when she tried to find out why. What a pity she wasn't a real witch. Can you imagine the fiendish revenge she might have devised for Messrs Ettricke and Frampton? It is to be hoped that Alder's apprentice, Henry Lawrence, did not adopt too many of his master's horse cures after he became qualified to practise as a blacksmith in 1806.

In 1807 Henry Lawrence married a local girl, Dorothy Clarke. The Bere Regis parish register also records the christening of two of their children, Ann in 1808, and John in 1810. A third child, William, was christened in Affpuddle in 1816, but by 1832 Henry and his family had moved again and were living in Studland. In that year, Ann Lawrence married a Studland man called Joseph Foot. By 1838 Henry's name was appearing regularly in the Bankes Estate stewards' accounts for services rendered as a blacksmith, earning from them about the same amount a year as his brother William. In 1844 Henry's son William married a Studland girl called Annabelle Dyer. Her father was a sailor and so was her new husband. So the Lawrences had a young seaman in the family. Think how useful that would have been if you were running smuggled goods across the Channel?

What of the other Lawrences? What was happening 15 miles away in Briantspuddle during this time? William says not a word about it, but he cannot have been unaffected by the death of his father John in 1822, or of his mother Ann in 1826? And he cannot have been ignorant of the death in 1826 of John Ridout, his sister Elizabeth's husband, or of the fact that, two years later, she married Wareham-born widower Henry Courtenay? And then there was Sally, his other sister...

In 1820, Sally (also known as Sarah) Lawrence married Affpuddle man Edward Legg. It was a fertile union and by 1833, they had five children. Henry and Elizabeth Courtenay, who also lived in Affpuddle, had about seven children between them. Legg and Courtenay were farm labourers and they were finding that, as their families were growing larger, their wages were becoming smaller. Having suffered cuts for several years running, their money had been reduced from nine shillings a week to seven. At the end of 1833, facing a further cut to six shillings a week, they were desperate. Then, one day, just before Christmas, at about 7 o'clock in the evening, Edward Legg heard a knock at the window of his cottage. He looked up. Outside were James Brine and James Hammett, two labourers from a neighbouring village. They beckoned to him and he went out to talk to them. They told him they were gathering men together to form a union with which to lobby their employers to prevent further wage cuts. A meeting was planned and they invited him to it. He asked who else was going and, when told that his brother-in-law Henry Courtenay was one of them, he agreed to join them. They all went to Thomas Stanfield's house in Tolpuddle where a formal ceremony was performed admitting them into a union formed by George and James Loveless, literate labourers and lay preachers in the Methodist Church. An oath was administered. Since 1824 forming a trade union had been legal but, under the Mutiny Act of 1797, the administering of an oath was not.

The local magistrate at the time was none other than James Frampton. He heard about the meeting and, already concerned about the unrest caused by the depressed economic situation in his area, consulted the Government who gave him a free hand to deal with it. On 22 February 1834, in Tolpuddle, a handbill appeared warning the labourers that by joining 'illegal societies or unions, to which they bind themselves by unlawful oaths' they would be committing a felony. It was signed by nine magistrates, including James Frampton, his son Henry, his brother-in-law C R Wollaston, and his correspondent from Corfe Castle, the obliging Rev John Morton Colson. The next day Frampton had six of the men who were at the meeting in Stanfield's house arrested and charged with committing a felony. They were George and James Loveless, Thomas and John Stanfield, James Hammett and James Brine.

The six Tolpuddle men were tried at Dorchester by a jury consisting mostly of farmers. They were found guilty. Before passing sentence, the judge asked if they had anything to say. George Loveless handed him a piece of paper. On it were these words:

> "My Lord, if we had violated any law, it was not done intention-
> ally; we have injured no man's reputation, character, person or
> property; we were uniting together to preserve ourselves, our wives
> and our children from utter degradation and starvation. We chal-
> lenge any man or number of men, to prove that we have acted, or
> intended to act, different from the above statement."

Having read this the judge sentenced Loveless and each of his co-defenders to seven years transportation.

The leading witness at their trial was Edward Legg, William Lawrence's brother-in-law. Whether Legg gave evidence against the men voluntarily or because, as one of Frampton's impoverished and starving labourers, it was in the best interests of his young family to do, is not known.

Frampton got the verdict he wanted but, in doing so, he created a backlash against the Government. There was outrage at the injustice meted out to the men and a campaign was mounted by trade unionists to free them. Petitions came in from all over the country, the signatures nearly totalling a million. The Government prevaricated for two years but was eventually forced to yield to public pressure: in 1836, the six men were granted a full and free pardon and brought back from Australia.

The 'Tolpuddle Martyrs' returned to their village, but nothing had changed. James Frampton was still in Moreton, still a threat and, as he was unlikely to leave they, like William Lawrence before them, left instead. Assisted by funds collected for their benefit, they made new lives for themselves first in Essex then in Canada. Only James Hammett remained in Tolpuddle. The Leggs continued to live in Affpuddle, and so did the Courtenays. They were still there when James Frampton died in 1855.

Was William Lawrence as unaware of the problems facing his sisters' families in Affpuddle in the early 1830s as his silence in his autobiography suggests? Or was he, yet again, being prudent by saying nothing about it? At the time he dictated his story, he was an old man living rent free due to the goodwill of the Bankes family, who occupied the same powerful niche in Studland society as the Framptons did in Moreton and Affpuddle. In the circumstances, would he have wanted it known that a family association linked him with the working class unrest that had culminated in the infamous trail of the Tolpuddle Martyrs?

The Bankes Family. How strong was Lawrence's connection with them? When was it made? The 1841 Census supplies us with the first real evidence of a personal acquaintanceship between William and a member of the family because, at the time it was taken, George Bankes was in Studland in Lawrence's company.

George Bankes (1787-1856) was William John Bankes' brother. He was younger by only a year, but they were very different characters. George was a family man. Kingston Lacy, the Bankes' family home, was very much William John's house, as the modern visitor will discover; George Bankes preferred Studland.

In 1822 a Studland tenant called Thomas Rowe died and George Bankes took over his cottage, renting it from his father's estate. By 1841 he was renting another two parcels of land in the parish. In that year William John, having been committed for trial for a homosexual offence, fled the country leaving the estate in George's hands. It was then that George decided to build for himself and his growing family a marine villa - the Manor House (now the Manor Hotel) - on one of his Studland plots. The Tithe Map of 1840 shows the site devoid of buildings, so work must have begun after that date. By 1847, however, we know it was largely finished because, in that year, George Bankes employed builders to make alterations and improvements to it. At the time, William Lawrence was the village publican.

Since 1827 at least, the Studland public house - the *New Inn* - had been run by George Damon. It was a small establishment - a cottage and garden - rented from the Bankes Estate. When Damon died in 1844, William Lawrence took it over, renaming it the *Wellington Inn*. The rent was £8 a year and that first year, Lawrence fell into arrears. His debt was cleared by the end of 1846 and thereafter he paid regularly. He seems to have made a success of the venture. Was that due to the 'import' of cheap spirits? - Studland's South Beach is just across the field from where the public house once stood - or was it due to good 'pub grub'?

'Pub lunches' are not a new concept; Lawrence was supplying them to his customers in the mid-19th Century. In 1847 and 1848, young William Masters Hardy was one of those employed by George Bankes to make alterations to the Manor House. In his book *Old Swanage; or Purbeck Past and Present* (1910), he recalls how he and the other workmen were sent down to the *Wellington Inn* to partake of their meals and the ale which Mr Bankes allowed each workman and boy, one pint being given to a man and half a pint to each boy. Although one hour, the usual time, was allowed for dinner, Hardy goes on, it sometimes took an hour and a half to get through the meal, especially when the old soldier was in an anecdotal mood, and related some of his thrilling and desperate adventures. Hardy shrewdly points out that Lawrence was retailing his beer along with his yarns and relates how, after Lawrence had told them a story about a new polish invented by a soldier to give a lustrous shine to the Duke of Wellington's boots, the glow of pride which spread over his countenance was every bit as bright as the leather on Wellington's boots. "It was a triumph of exalted genius," said Hardy.

Lawrence was 57 at the time. Three years later, Henry Lawrence's wife Dorothy died. Three years after that, in 1853, Clotilde died. Henry died in 1856, followed six weeks' later by George Bankes at Kingston Lacy. Also in 1856,

Lawrence (who was then 66) gave up the *Wellington Inn*, handing over to Moses Gould of Kingswood Farm, who changed the name back to the *New Inn*. It cannot have been long afterwards that he dictated his autobiography.

From 1857, Lawrence lived alone in a rent-free cottage belonging to the Bankes Estate. It is from this last phase of his life that we have our second eye-witness account of him. In about 1923, George Nugent Bankes' sister - who was by then Mrs John E Acland - wrote a precis of Lawrence's autobiography in an exercise book. At the end she added an anecdote of her own, describing how, as a child, she used to visit Lawrence in his little cottage and talk to him. One day she asked him "Why does your head shake so, Sergeant?" To which he replied, "Well Missy, it was like this - when I was fighting Boney a cannon ball took my head off and when the doctors put it on again they put in on crooked."

William Lawrence died in December 1869 at the age of 80. He was buried in St Nicholas's Churchyard in the same plot at Clotilde, marked today by a large and distinctive gravestone. Although William and Clotilde had no children, some writers of books about the Isle of Purbeck, have implied the existence of a daughter. The story goes like this:

After Waterloo, William met and married Clotilde Clairet and a daughter was born to them. After three years in the garrison at St Germain, being suddenly recalled to England, they decided to leave the girl in France in the care of Clotilde's brother. Instead of looking after the child himself, the brother put her in an orphanage but continued to receive the money the Lawrences sent for her support. When the girl was thirteen, and the Lawrences were settled in England, they sent for her, but she could not be found.

This tale first appeared in Woodward's *In and Around the Isle of Purbeck* for which one of the author's sources was Viola Bankes, the great-grandaughter of George Bankes. She may have been the source of the story, but it isn't true. Clotilde and William cannot possibly have met before October 1815 when the 40th Regiment were sent to St Germain where they were in barracks for three *months* not three years. Even if Clotilde had conceived on the very day she met Lawrence, she could not have been more than 6 months pregnant when they married in April 1816, at which time they were in Cambrai, 100 miles from St Germain. Why would they have sent their baby 100 miles away to St Germain when Lawrence - legally married to Clotilde - was entitled to take both her and his child back to England with him? And why would they have placed the baby in the charge of one of Clotilde's two brothers (aged 18 and 16 respectively at the time) when neither was married, and both lived at home with her parents?

No, there was no daughter, but there were daughters aplenty born to William's brothers and sisters. And sons. A determined search of the Parish Registers would bring to light in the Purbeck and Dorchester areas, many of their descendants.

In the Introduction it was pointed out that, for the first 27 years of his life, William Lawrence was a contemporary of Jane Austen; for the last 29 he lived contemporaneously with another English novelist - Thomas Hardy. William Lawrence's people were not Jane Austen's people, but they were Thomas Hardy's.

Thomas Hardy was born in 1840 in Higher Bockhampton, six miles from Briantspuddle. Midway between the two hamlets is Puddletown, where William sent his brother to get ale to celebrate his homecoming during his leave in 1817. Puddletown is the 'Weatherbury' of *Far from the Madding Crowd*; set in the 1840s. It is unlikely that Hardy met Lawrence but he may have learned of him when researching *The Trumpet Major* (1880), his novel of the Napoleonic period.

Hardy did not write about William Lawrence, but fortunately for us, William Lawrence wrote about himself. He left us his own story. And what a story it is! But what is it a story of? A hero? That is how Lawrence was described by George Nugent Bankes in 1886, but it does not appear to be how Lawrence saw himself. Too often in his youth he was a victim of circumstance, trapped inside lethal situations which denied him any reasonable choices. Does a man choose to be flogged by the army for being absent without leave rather than flogged by his master for staying out late? Does he prefer to be half-starved as a soldier to being half-starved as an apprentice? Does he want to be shot at by the French for being brave, instead of shot by the British for being a coward? Is it a matter of preference to risk being maimed for life by a mine for being too adventurous because being timorous would earn the ignominious maiming of the lash? These were the dilemmas Lawrence faced, so what were the qualities he displayed in coming to terms with them?

In my opinion William Lawrence was a resilient and resourceful character whose courage sprang from straightforward commonsense. If he displayed intelligence in understanding the situations in which he found himself, and judgement in dealing with them, it is because he learned to view them realistically. It is that realism, that basic integrity, that makes his account of his years as a soldier so timeless and so fresh. What a tragic loss it is then to our archive of social history that he felt constrained from writing about the last 50 years of his life with the same unfettered vision he used on the first thirty.

Aspects of Lawrence's experience do have modern parallels. In recent times former prisoners-of-war and political hostages, having survived incarceration and brutalisation in Iraq and Beirut have returned home to Britain to find themselves described as heroes. To this they firmly shake their heads. "We're not heroes," one said of himself and his colleague. "Heroes are those who have, and make, choices; we had our choices taken away. Our story is not about heroism, but about survival."

Survival. Isn't that what William Lawrence's story is really about?

NOTES

CHAPTER 1

1. The Register for St Lawrence's Church, Affpuddle, records that he was baptised on 28 Nov 1790.
2. Briantspuddle, on the River Piddle, used to be called Bryant's Piddle, and that is what Lawrence always called it. At that time, the neighbouring villages of Affpuddle, Tolpuddle and Turnerspuddle were similarly named. I can only assume that the names were changed by Victorians offended by a few too many piddles.
3. There had been Lawrences in Affpuddle Parish for generations, one family being descended from the Elizabethan knight, Sir Edward Lawrence of Creech Grange. These noble Lawrences had a marriage alliance with the Washington's of Sulgrave, Northamptonshire, from whom George Washington was descended. It is rather less likely that were allied to the humble Briantspuddle Lawrences. William's father, John Lawrence, was an illiterate farm labourer and was a widower of 48 when he married Ann Hooper in 1782.
4. Because Ann Hooper was 20 years younger than her husband she was fertile enough to still be bearing him children when he was an old man. The youngest was born when John was 62, about the age that William sat down to write his memoirs! The children were Henry 1783, John 1787, Samuel 1789, William 1790, George 1792, Elizabeth 1794, and Sally 1796. There were two other children - Samuel, 1784-1788, and John 1786-1787. Both died in infancy and were buried as paupers. In the late 19th Century it was common for parents to give new babies the names of brothers or sisters who had died.
5. The apprenticeship was paid for by a charity set up by the Frampton family of Moreton to help the children of the poor in the parishes of Moreton, Affpuddle and Turnerspuddle. The agreement was dated 24 March 1804, when William was 13. The amount paid was £15 and Henry Bush is described as a stonemason of Swanage Parish. It is possible that Bush lived, not in Studland village, but at Ulwell, midway between Studland and Swanage at the foot of the downs. Half of Ulwell was in Studland Parish and half in Swanage Parish. Bush's father certainly lived in Ulwell. His name, and the names of other family members, are recorded in the parish registers of both Studland and Swanage.
6. This may have been Thomas Linnington, another Affpuddle youth.
7. The indentures were held by the charity's trustees in Moreton. William would not have known this.
8. King's Wood is a still a wood. It is on the hill on the north side of Nine Barrow Down. Just over a mile from Ulwell, it overlooks Kingswood Farm. Beyond is a panoramic view of Poole Harbour.
9. Beer of a weak or inferior quality.
10. In the early 19th Century, Poole was a thriving port. Its merchants had established important trading links with Newfoundland.
11. South Deep is a navigable stretch of water in Poole Harbour, just north of the

Goathorn Peninsula. At this time, the stone which was quarried in Purbeck was carried by wagons to Ower and Goathorn, and there loaded onto barges.

12. In the Civil Defence Census of 1803, there is no Mrs Bush. Henry Bush's name appears alongside that of Thomas Linnington, who was his other apprentice, and Ann Curtis. In 1812, a couple named as Henry and Ann Bush became the parents of Sarah, who was christened in Swanage. A record of their marriage cannot be traced. Is it possible that, at the time William was his apprentice, Ann Curtis was Henry's common law wife.

13. The *Horse and Groom* still exists, trading under the same name.

14. Dorchester in 9 miles further on from Wareham than Briantspuddle. Despite the reassurance William had given the landlady at the *Horse and Groom*, he had by-passed his home village.

CHAPTER 2

1. It was so common for apprentices to run away and join the army that official forms acknowledged the fact. One was headed "State of Balance of Effects and Credits or Debts of the Non-Commissioned officers, drummers, fifers and privates of the — Regiment of — who have died or deserted, or have been delivered up in consequence of being apprentices."

2. Almost certainly James Frampton of Moreton, the local landowner and one of the trustees of the charity which had paid for William's apprenticeship. In 1834, Frampton was the driving force behind the arrest, conviction and transportation of the men who became known as the Tolpuddle Martyrs.

3. At this time the British army was made up entirely of 'volunteers'. Enlistment was often the only way a felon could escape a term of imprisonment. Those with a nautical background, eg fishermen-cum-smugglers, were pressed into the navy.

4. He enlisted on 19 Feb 1805 and was paid a bounty of £2.12s.6d.

5. June 1805.

6. The 40th Regt were barracked along the coasts of Kent and Sussex because of the fear of invasion after May 1803, when England had again gone to war with France.

7. By January 1806 Lawrence was in the 1st Battalion, in Captain Balfour's company.

8. In August 1806, the Regiment marched from Bexhill to Portsea barracks.

CHAPTER 3

1. Smythies (History of the 40th Regiment) says they embarked on 16 Sept 1806, but government documents give the date as 9 October. Lt-Col Gore Browne commanded the regiment which consisted of 2 majors, 10 captains, 16 lieutenants, 8 ensigns, 6 staff, 54 sergeants, 22 drummers, and 1000 men. They were part of a force of 2996 men under the command of Sir Samuel Auchmuty. Young Harry Smith (whose autobiography was published in 1901) was also with the fleet. In his diary he listed the ships in the convoy as HMS *Ardent*, *Unicorn* (frigate), *Daphne* (20-gun

ship), *Pheasant* and *Charwell* (sloops of war), a fleet of 25 transports, store ship, and merchant ship.

2.   Harry Smith, writing on 9 Nov said that there was a fine breeze until 12th (October) when they were becalmed in the Bay of Biscay, but that on the 13th a breeze sprung up which increased into a gale and blew 'dreadful hard' with the sea like 'mountains'. He also states that on the 18th, when it blew hard again, the *Daphne*, and a transport with 150 men of the 40th Regt parted from the convoy in the night.

3.   Collins Dictionary defines the 'equinoctial line' as the 'celestial equator'.

4.   Either Maj John Dalrymple or Maj D Campbell. 'Grog' was rum and water.

5.   They reached Rio at the end of December 1806 where Auchmuty learned that the British expeditionary force in Buenos Aires had been overwhelmed in August and that Beresford and his men were prisoners of the Spanish. The situation had changed: Buenos Aires had to be retaken, but first Auchmuty had to take Montevideo. His fleet arrived at Maldonado on 5 Jan 1807.

6.   Auchmuty had sailed with 3000 men, but officers were not included in that total therefore, after the rendez-vous, the number may well have totalled 5000.

7.   On 6 Feb 1807, in his despatch to William Wyndham, Secretary of State for War and the Colonies, Auchmuty says the landing was on 16 Jan 1807, in a small bay to the west of the Caretas rock, 9 miles from Montevideo.

8.   Lt Fitzpatrick was one of them; Major Campbell and Captain Rogers were wounded.

9.   On 19 Jan 1807, Auchmuty's men took up a position about 2 miles from the citadel.

10.   20 Jan 1807.

11.   Auchmuty said on 6 Feb that the Spanish force which attacked was 6000 strong, that 3 companies of the 40th Regiment, headed by Major Campbell, charged the head of the column - 'great numbers fell on both sides'. He said the Spanish column gave way under an outflanking movement by the Light Battalion and Rifle Corps and 'were pursued with great slaughter'. Auchmuty put the enemy casualties at 1500 of which 200-300 were killed. British casualties were, he said, 'comparatively trifling'. There is a wide discrepancy between Lawrence's 'thousands' of Spanish killed and Auchmuty's 'hundreds'. Did Lawrence mean 'hundreds', or had Auchmuty dramatically revised the figure down in despatches to London to disguise the fact that a massacre of Spanish troops had taken place? Lawrence's estimate of casualties are, as you will discover, usually quite accurate.

12.   Terminology for siege warfare tended to be French. A 'gabion' was a wickerwork basket filled with stones or earth to provide cover for troops in a siege. 'Fascines' were bundles of long sticks used in the construction of embankments and fortifications.

13.   3 Feb 1807

14.   Captain Charles Renny commanded the 40th Regt's light infantry of which Lawrence - still only 16 and therefore not yet fully grown - was one.

15.   In this context a 'forlorn hope' was a small group of soldiers, usually led by a junior officer, who preceded the main assault of a fortified town, equipped with ladders to scale the breach and the walls.

16.   Auchmuty ordered the attack for an hour before daylight. It was very dark and the breach could not at first be discerned because it had been barricaded with hides.

Renny found it but was struck down while mounting it. His soldiers rushed through and forced their way into the town. The Rifle Corps, Light Infantry, Grenadiers and 38th Regiment led the assault. The rest of the 40th under Maj Dalrymple, along with the 37th Regt, were in support. Of the 40th, Maj Dalrymple, 5 other officers and 112 men were killed; and 17 officers and 400 men wounded. Sgt William Luxton was commended for his bravery in gathering up in his hands a live shell, the fuse still burning, and throwing it over the parapet of the battery - occupied by members of the 40th's light company - where it had landed.

17. Auchmuty gave the total as 2,000.
18. Don Pasquil Ruis Huidobro.
19. Auchmuty reports that on the morning after the surrender the town was quiet and that women were peacefully walking the streets. He admits that there had been some disorder, owing to the inhabitants 'giving' liquor to the troops, but it had been of 'trifling consequence and soon checked'.
20. These prisoners were soon to be used to bargain for the release of General Beresford and his men, who were prisoners of the Spanish in Buenos Aires.

CHAPTER 4

1. Henry Goodfellow was a sergeant in Captain Porter's company, but had been a corporal in Lawrence's.
2. Writing to William Wyndham on 26 April 1807, Auchmuty refers to this incident, informing him that there had been desertions because of efforts to 'entice' the men from their colours. The two Spaniards were executed on 27 April.
3. River Plate
4. Colonia del Sacramenta was taken just before 20 March 1807 by a force which included a detachment of 6 companies of the 40th, commanded by Lt-Col Denis Pack of the 71st Regiment. Pack had been with Beresford's contingent in Buenos Aires in July 1806, had been taken prisoner there in August, but had escaped (with Beresford).
5. A *cheval de frise* was a barrier made of blades, often used to block breaches.
6. The attack was made at 1am on 22 April. Auchmuty says the attackers were pursued to the village of Real, 3 miles from Colonia. In May the detachment was reinforced by the remainder of the 40th.
7. On 8 June 1807, in a despatch to General Whitelocke (who had recently taken over command of the army from Auchmuty), Pack says: 'Having obtained information on Saturday evening last that the enemy had taken post at St Pedro, 12 miles from this, I resolved upon moving to attack him, and commenced my march accordingly at 3 o'clock the next morning, with a force amounting to 1013 rank and file.'
8. Pack described the enemy as being 1000 strong, situated on an eminence, their front ranks secured by a deep and marshy river which the troops crossed, many up to their middles in water, before advancing. The enemy cavalry gave way but the enemy infantry stood their ground until Pack's men were within a few paces, when they fled in disorder. 120 of the enemy were killed, 105 taken prisoner. Pack recommended

the 40th Regiment to General Whitelocke for their bravery.

9.   Lt-Col Pack.

10.   Those severely injured in the explosion were Major Gardner and 14 men of the Rifle
       Corps, one of whom had died by 8 June when Pack wrote to Whitelocke describing
       the incident in ambiguous terms. He called it an 'unfortunate explosion' of 2
       ammunition wagons taken from the enemy, but then adds 'which it was necessary
       to destroy after the action was over'. It was almost certainly an accident.

11.   The casualties suffered by the 40th at San Pedro were 4 privates killed, and 1
       sergeant and 19 rank and file soldiers wounded.

CHAPTER 5

1.   Whitelocke arrived in Montevideo on 11 May 1807, General Craufurd and his men
       on 12 June.

2.   Numbering 7,800 men.

3.   At Ensenada de Barragon, a small bay 30 miles to the east of Buenos Aires, on 28
       June 1807.

4.   Whitelocke described the march - going through countryside 'much intersected by
       swamps and deep muddy rivulets' - as 'fatiguing'.

5.   The 40th, ordered to remain in the village of Reduction, did not take part.

6.   The battle for Buenos Aires began on 5 July. Sections of Whitelocke's army were
       in advance of the main body and fought their way into the city but, being separated,
       communication broke down. Troops, used to fighting on open ground, found
       themselves isolated in the streets of the town. They became entrapped and some
       surrendered to the Spanish forces of Liniers. Whitelocke, faced with the prospect
       of renewing the attack with the rest of his army, and endangering further the lives
       of those already in the city, decided to enter into negotiations with Liniers. A
       ceasefire was proclaimed on 6 July.

7.   A treaty of capitulation was signed on 7 July. The British agreed to leave
       Montevideo within two months.

8.   Montevideo was evacuated on 9 Sept 1807, bringing an end to the British military
       engagement in South America. Whitelocke was blamed for the defeat and faced a
       court-martial when he returned home, a convenient scapegoat for the failure of an
       ill-conceived project. His doubts about the expedition, and of the tenability of the
       British position, were clearly expressed to William Wyndham on 20 June when he
       argued that the conflict had arisen out of individual interest not out of 'great national
       interest'. He said that the numbers of troops available to him were insufficient to
       impose the British Government's will on a Spanish population which was not only
       many, many times more populous, but universally hostile.

9.   This incident is true, but almost certainly took place on the way home from North
       America in 1815, not on the way home from South America in 1807 (see Chapter
       22).

10.   They marched to Bandon, Co Cork where they were joined by 250 men of the 2nd
       battalion, then they went on to Fermoy, then Limerick, and finally back to the cove
       of Cork, where Col James Kemmis assumed command.

CHAPTER 6

1.   Other sources give the number as 10,000.

2.   In Spain.

3.   On 8 Aug 1808.

4.   General Brent Spencer with 5,000 troops.

5.   On 17 Aug 1808. One man in the 40th was killed, several wounded. They marched to Lourinha where they were assigned to Maj-Gen Ronald Ferguson's brigade.

6.   The soldiers of the 4th Division, of which Lawrence was one, were known as 'honeysuckers' for their skill in robbing beehives. Wellington himself caught one soldier red-handed but did not have the heart to punish him. (Longford)

7.   The Battle of Vimeiro took place on 21 Aug 1808.

8.   A tactic of the French army was to place daring skirmishers before its bodies of Grenadiers. At Vimeiro, to counter the threat, Wellesley did the same.

9.   The 40th lost 13 rank and file killed, 60 wounded. They had fought, like the rest of Wellesley's infantry, in a thin line just 2 ranks deep, thereby enabling the men in the second rank to use their muskets as effectively as those in the front. The French troops were formed into rectangular columns, 30 men broad 42 deep; this meant that the muskets of the men in the rear could not be brought into play. They had suffered because of their lack of flexibility.

10.   The day after Vimeiro, the army leaders (who were now General Sir Hugh Dalrymple and General Sir Harry Burrard) signed a 48-hour armistice, ratified on 31 August as the Convention at Cintra. Burrard, on the field of battle at Vimeiro, had been given the opportunity to pursue the defeated French army and destroy it, but he had declined. Now he put his signature to a document allowing the repatriation from Portugal, in British ships, of the entire French army, their plunder and their arms. It was to incense public opinion at home. Portugal had indeed been liberated from the French, but Spain had not.

11.   On 24 Sept, the 40th mustered at Monte Santo camp, and on 24 Oct at the Benedictine convent.

12.   The Convention of Cintra. Wellesley left at the beginning of October. Sir John Moore was left in charge of the army in Lisbon.

13.   The 40th moved to Elvas in Nov 1808.

14.   On 6 Oct 1808, Sir John Moore had been ordered into northern Spain with 20,000 troops, leaving 10,000 behind to protect Portugal. Faced by a French onslaught he had retreated, and was killed at Corunna on 16 Jan 1809.

15.   The 40th Regiment, 871 men strong, arrived in Seville in February. They were there on 22 Mar 1809 when Spanish-speaking Major E C Cocks complained in a letter home that he was hearing his own language because the 40th were quartered in the city.

16.   Probably James Kemmis.

17.   He was 18.

18.   Discipline in the British army was brutal. 750-1000 lashes was not an uncommon sentence and, all too often, resulted in the death of the man being 'punished'. Wellesley's soldiers were all 'volunteers' and on more than one occasion he called

them the 'scum of the earth' who needed the threat of the triangle to keep them in order. 'People talk of their enlisting from their fine military feeling; all stuff - no such thing,' he said. 'Some of our men enlist from having got bastard children, some for minor offences, many more for drink.' No allowances were paid to the men's dependants so, if a soldier was sent abroad without them, his family had to fend for themselves. Irish militiamen's families fared so badly that it astonished Wellington that the men enlisted at all. A man who volunteered for a few guineas to get drunk with must, he said, be 'the very worst members of society' (Longford p322). Wellington came from a privileged background; is that why he had so little understanding of the degrading lack of choice that men - and youths like William Lawrence - experienced at the lowest end of the social scale?

19.   Lawrence had been little more than a boy when he enlisted and was therefore ideal material for the light infantry, but by 1809 he had grown into a man. He was 18 now and, at over 6 feet tall, better suited to the Grenadier company, which selected men for their height and their strength. His discharge papers at the Public Record Office which describe him as having hazel eyes and a sallow complexion.

CHAPTER 7

1.   Soon after 21 April 1809.
2.   This may have been Mr Gordon of Xeres. In her book about Edward Charles Cocks, Julia Page writes that in December 1809, a Mr Gordon, reknowned for his hospitality to travellers, took Cocks and his commanding officer over his farm and into his wine vaults to sample his sherry, before directing them to a nearby Carthusian convent to view its collection of Murillos.
3.   Before the battle, 2000 Spanish troops were panicked by enemy musket fire into firing a mass salvo at French troops too far away to be harmed. Observing this, Wellesley turned to one of his liaison officers: 'If they will but fire as well to-morrow, the day is our own; but as there seems nobody to fire at just now, I wish you would stop it.' Then they fled. 'Look at the ugly hole those fellows have left,' he added, and ordered it to be filled. (Longford p193).
4.   British casualties were put at 5000, the French at 7000. The 40th lost 16 killed. Capt Colqhoun and 90 men were severely wounded.
5.   Lawrence is referring to disagreements between the two generals: Wellesley had wanted to attack Victor on 21 July but old Cuesta did not. Cuesta had wanted to attack Victor on 24 July but Wellesley did not.
6.   When King Joseph's army threatened him, Cuesta decamped and rejoined Welling-ton leaving 1500 wounded in French hands.
7.   Wellesley had trouble getting food for his army, which caused tension with his Spanish allies who were supposed to be supplying it. The truth was that there was little on the land to start with, and considerably less after the French army had passed through. Relations with the Spanish were not improved by the fact that Wellesley was withdrawing from their country, or that his starving men supplemented their meagre rations by plundering from the local people.

8. E C Cocks was probably more accurate in ascribing the sickness to the men drinking foul water, fresh being so scarce. The illness may have been dysentery, known then called Walcheren fever, but malaria was another affliction suffered by the troops in the Peninsula.

9. There were 2 major Spanish fortresses on the border with Portugal - Badajoz in the south, and Ciudad Rodrigo in the north. Both were strategically important and each had a Portuguese counterpart about 10 miles away - Elvas and Almeida. Badajoz was to change hands several times during the war, but after Talavera it was under Allied control. The 40th arrived there in Sept 1809.

10. One of the 40th's surgeons, Charles Boutflower, kept a diary between 1809 and 1813. He records that the Elvas convents were filled with great numbers of sick soldiers. On 22 Oct, he wrote: 'Sickness has constantly prevailed in the Army to an alarming extent, there being seldom less than 8000 sick on an average, of which number the deaths have been most afflicting'.

11. He had returned to Badajoz by 3 Nov 1809 for that is when the 40th marched to Olivenza.

12. On 8 Aug 1809, the Spanish Junta made him captain-general of the Spanish forces.

CHAPTER 8

1. The move was made earlier - 3 Nov 1809. Boutflower said Olivenza was a neat Spanish town where most of the inhabitants were Portuguese because it had formerly belonged to Portugal.

2. Samuel Moon had been a drummer in the same company as Lawrence.

3. Lewis Phelps. He too had been ill at Elvas. He was transferred to the 2nd Battalion on 24 July 1811.

4. They left Olivenza on 17 Dec and marched 250 miles to Guarda via Estremoz, Abrantes, Thomar, Leiria, Pombal, Condeixa, Coimbra, Melo and Celorico. They reached Guarda about 20 Jan 1810. There both the regiment and the army were strengthened by arrivals from England. There too Boutflower records the hanging of 3 soldiers of the 27th Regt for burglary, which Wellington had made a capital offence. A few weeks later, a local family was found murdered, the victims of soldiers who had nothing to lose by taking such a drastic measure to conceal their identities as burglars.

5. Marshal André Massena, commander of the French Army of Portugal.

6. Boutflower, writing from Guarda: 'We amuse ourselves chiefly at cricket' and 'from the ground where we play can distinctly see the fire from the garrison of Almeida'.

7. The explosion was an accident. Hundreds died and the town centre was destroyed.

8. In July 1810.

9. General Sir Galbraith Lowry Cole.

CHAPTER 9

1. On 28 Oct, the day after the battle, they were ordered to Coimbra.
2. Wellington conducted a scorched-earth policy. At Coimbra, stores that could not be carried were destroyed, and abandoned houses set on fire. British soldiers freed the inmates of prisons and asylums. Kincaid, in his *Adventures in the Rifle Brigade* said: 'The civil authorities, in making their own hurried escape, had totally forgotten that they had left a jail full of rogues'. When the French army arrived, they looted what little remained. Massena left 5000 of his sick and wounded in the hospital, guarded by a few able-bodied men but, as soon as he had departed, a strong Portuguese force took the town back.
3. The 40th were in the village of Filileira, near Sobral, from 11 Oct 1810.
4. Massena's communication with, and supplies from, France were hindered by mountain guerillas in Spain. His soldiers suffered, as Wellington intended, and many deserted to the English lines, about 50 a day according to Boutflower.
5. Boutflower says that this was stopped, 'it being justly considered that the Simplicity of our Fellows was no match for the Cunning of a Frenchman'! As Lawrence is about to demonstrate, soldiers didn't come more cunning than the grenadiers of the 40th!
6. Wellington was aware of his soldiers' plundering. In a despatch dated 11 Jan 1811, he pleaded for a reform of the recruiting system to improve the quality of his men.
7. Massena's army decamped in a fog on the night of 14 Nov, leaving a line of straw dummies, with shakos on poles, to look like sentries.
8. The Portuguese peasantry starved too. On the retreat of the French, Kincaid reported seeing starved men stalking amid the wreck of their friends and property like so many skeletons 'permitted to leave their graves for the purpose of wreaking vengeance on their oppressors'.
9. At a place called 'Yambuza' (Azambuja?) where they remained until 6 March 1811.
10. So it seems that the Portuguese farmer was not reimbursed for his stolen dollars after all?

CHAPTER 10

1. 14 March 1811. Boutflower says that every house was burnt to the ground. On 16 March he wrote that the wretched inhabitants of the region were returning to their destroyed dwellings: 'The enormities committed on the property and persons of these poor people by the Enemy can scarcely be recited with the expectation of gaining belief'. In his account, Capt Kincaid of the Rifle Brigade is more graphic.
2. Lawrence's memory seems to have failed him. Official regimental documents record that William Halfhead was killed in South America in 1807, not at Cazal Nova in 1811.
3. They reached Portalegre, which Boutflower says had a 'beautiful cathedral and the principal Cloth Manufactory of the Kingdom', on 22 March.
4. They arrived on 25 March.

CHAPTER 11

1. In the 1886 edition, the sequence of events in this chapter was inaccurate. Lawrence remembered it as Campo Maior-Badajoz-Olivenza-Badajoz-Albuera. Boutflower's diary gives it more accurately as Campo Maior-Olivenza-Badajoz-Albuera.
2. 16 April 1811.
3. Lt-Col Harcourt was in command of the 40th at the time.
4. On 11 March 1811.
5. The 40th were assigned to Fort St Christoval, an outwork of Badajoz. Ground was broken on 8 May, the attack taking place on the 10th. Boutflower said the French succeeded in taking possession for a moment 'and were proceeding to destroy the Work when they were charged by the picquets and compelled to retreat. Unfortunately our troops pursued them with their wonted ardour to the very Walls, where they were exposed to a most destructive fire of shell, shot and musketry', which killed and wounded 400. 'It was one of the most painful days of my life,' said the surgeon. Of the 40th, 58 men were killed. Lt-Col Harcourt, and Captains Heyland and Wood, were wounded along with 250 of their men.
6. The 40th did not arrive on the battlefield until 17 May when the action was over, therefore Lawrence took no part in it. The account he gives is second hand.
7. Colonel (later Sir) Henry Hardinge, (1785-1856).
8. Boutflower says 'On our arrival on the Field of Combat a Scene most horrible that the imagination can conceive presented itself. The ground was covered with the dead and dying'. 'I have been so completely horrified at the dreadful scenes I have lately been compelled to witness, that they have given me a disgust for the Army I never before entertained'. The Allies lost 4000 men out of 10,000, the French 7,000 out of 24,000. The dead, stripped of their clothes, were buried, but a year later their bones littered the ground.
9. The 40th did not return to the siege of Badajoz. The allies had to withdraw from the environs of Badajoz when the French army under Marshall Soult again advanced on them. The French entered and relieved the town on 16 June, thus ending the second siege of Badajoz.

CHAPTER 12

1. The 40th were at Azenchal, several miles south-west of Albuera, until 11 June. It was so excessively hot that Boutflower feared for the men's health. He worried that if they fell sick again more would be lost through that than to the enemy.
2. Fuente Guinaldo, Wellington's headquarters, a few miles from Ciudad Rodrigo, which they reached on 24 Sept after a long and arduous march via Albuera, Elvas, Estremoz, Crato, Castelo Branco and Penamacor - which took 3 months to accomplish. At Crato, a detachment of 400 men from the 40th's 2nd battalion joined them. Many in the army fell ill, as Boutflower had feared. At one time 17,000 were sick, suffering from dysentery.
3. Atrocities were committed during the Peninsular War. Scorched earth policies were

practised by both armies causing shortages of food in areas where it was never plentiful in the first place. Desperately hungry and ruthless, some French soldiers tortured local peasants to try to get them to reveal food stores which they probably did not have, and/or killed them out of spite when none was found. Spanish painter Francisco Goya (1746-1828), depicted such scenes in a series of disturbing etchings called *The Disasters of War* (1810-14).

4.   George Harding.
5.   'thieving'.

CHAPTER 13

1.   Early in Oct, the 40th were moved to Gallegos, about 10 miles from Ciudad Rodrigo, where they were stationed until the end of 1811.
2.   During these operations, the 40th were posted in a village called Villa de Porco. It was midwinter, very cold, and the ground covered in snow. Their turn in the trenches was on the 9 Jan when 3 of their number were killed by artillery fire from the Convents of San Antonio and San Francisco; 13 were wounded. San Antonio was taken on the 13th by a party of the German Legion. That same day it was the 40th's turn in the trenches.
3.   This was the Convent of San Francisco. Three companies of the 40th stormed it on the night of 13 Jan.
4.   Maj-Gen Mackinnon was one of those killed.
5.   The storming of Ciudad Rodrigo involved the 3rd and Light Division, not the 4th Division, to which the 40th belonged. Napier was wounded and later had his arm amputated. General Robert Craufurd was mortally wounded, dying 4 days later.
6.   Boutflower on the aftermath at Ciudad Rodrigo: 'Gallant as are our soldiers when opposed to an Enemy, I fear they yield to no people on earth in their thirst for plunder'.
7.   The number of prisoners was 2000. The French lost just over 500 men killed and wounded, the Allies 1100.
8.   Most belonged to the Light Division. They were tried and those who could not prove that they were of previous good character - 11 of them - were shot. Their execution, witnessed by Harry Smith and described in his *Autobiography* (1901), was botched. Capt Kincaid reported, with some admiration, that one of the men demanded his arrears of pay before his execution.
9.   They returned to Villa de Porco and remained in the area of Gallegos until 10 Feb when they started their long march back to Badajoz.

CHAPTER 14

1.   They marched back to Badajoz the way they had come, via Castelo Branco and Elvas, arriving on 16 March.

2. The French force, consisting of about 1500 infantry, attacked on 19 March. They carried away about 500 tools.

3. A squadron of cavalry and a troop of artillery were held in readiness, and a better watch kept.

4. Fort Picurina, a detached bastion garrisoned by 300 French with 7 light guns.

5. This may have happened at Ciudad Rodrigo on 9 Jan when 3 men of the 40th were killed in the trenches, and about 13 wounded. Both Boutflower and Smythies record the incident at Ciudad Rodrigo, but not a similar one at Badajoz.

6. A fuse or line of gunpowder leading to a mine.

7. Only 80 got back, the rest were killed, captured, or drowned in the river Rivillas, which had been indundated by damming. The British loss was also high - 60% of the attacking force killed or wounded.

8. This is not so. In a letter dated 20 July 1813, Wellington stated that he did not summons Badajoz because French officers had orders not to surrender a place before it had been stormed. Boutflower on 2 April 1812: 'no idea is entertained of capitulation, indeed it is one of the fundamental rules of the Code Napoleon, that any Governor giving up a Fortress without standing the assault shall be shot'. On 5 April, he adds: 'The Town has not been summoned, and it is supposed it will not; it is said that Lord Wellington is unwilling to subject himself to an insolent reply'.

9. Each division was to be preceded to its breach by 500 men. The 4th Div was assigned to 2 breaches - at La Trinidad bastion, and another just to the west of it. Some of the men in the advance party carried ladders, others hay bags for throwing into the ditch to help soften the landing of those who fell.

10. The report may not have been true, but the expectation of the men was real. There were undoubtedly officers who not only accepted that plunder would take place after a siege, but regarded it as their men's legitimate reward for success. After the appalling conditions working in the trenches, their comrades killed and maimed by artillery fire, knowing from the experience at Ciudad Rodrigo that no better fate awaited them at the formidable breaches of Badajoz, the men needed something to look forward to. If plunder was their only heaven, they knew they had to go through hell to get it.

11. Other first-hand accounts suggest that the soldiers' mood was one of grim determination.

12. The obstacles were so formidable that there was confusion and order was lost. Capt Kincaid of the Light Div: 'The 5 succeeding hours were therefore passed in the most gallant and hopeless attempts on the part of individual officers, forming up 50 or 100 men at a time at the foot of the breach, and endeavouring to carry it by desperate bravery; and, fatal as it proved to each gallant band in succession yet, fast as one dissolved, another was formed'.

13. Was this Boutflower? It is possible, although he was not the only surgeon in the 40th. In his dairy, he makes little reference to his work so, without other first-hand evidence coming to light, there is no way of knowing.

14. There was no Lt Elland in the 40th, but there was a Lt Ayling, and he was indeed killed at Badajoz.

15. Filer did not survive the war either. A year later, on 29 April 1813, Charles Filer,

labourer of Coomesbury, who joined on 22 Aug 1807, became 'ineffective'. He died in hospital.

16. Wellington withdrew the 4th and Light Divisions from their breaches and ordered General Picton to take the castle with the 3rd Division.

17. When Wellington ordered the 4th and Light Divisions forward again, they found the breaches abandoned and got into the town over them.

18. The French General Phillipon had been in charge of Badajoz. He surrendered to Lord Fitzroy Somerset at Fort San Cristoval, just across the River Guadiana, a few hours later.

19. Cooper of the 7th Regt, part of the same division as the 40th, said that as soon as the obstructions were removed 'our maddened fellows rushed into the town by thousands. Wine shops were broken open and horrible scenes commenced. All order ceased. Plunder was the order of the night'. Pte Donaldson of the 94th: 'the gate leading into the town from the castle was opened and we were allowed to enter for the purpose of plundering it'. Capt Kincaid: 'our men were permitted to fall out, to enjoy themselves for the remainder of the day as a reward for having kept together for as long as they were wanted. The whole of the three divisions were by this time loose in the town, and the usual frightful scene of plunder commenced, which the officers thought it necessary to avoid for the moment by retiring to the camp'.

20. A pipe is a large cask of wine equal to 4 barrels.

21. Two Spanish sisters fled to the British camp from Badajoz, their ears bleeding where soldiers had ripped out their earrings. One, Juana Maria de los Dolores de Leon, was only 13 years old. In the camp she met Harry Smith whom she married less than a year later. Ladysmith in South Africa is named after her.

22. Kincaid states that the plunder and rioting were still going on after 24 hours and did not cease until 8 April when Wellington sent in a Portuguese brigade to stand at arms in the great square. There a gallows was erected and, Kincaid says, several miscreants hanged, but another witness - Capt Robert Blakeney of the 28th - says no executions took place. Later, on 15 April, Boutflower made this comment: 'The Army is far from healthy, or rather that part of it employed in the late Siege; the dreadful weather, aided by the horrid intemperance that took place, is making a melancholy ravage amongst the men; till drunkenness becomes a punishable crime, a British Army in the Peninsula never can be properly effective'.

23. 72 officers and 963 men were killed, and 306 officers and 3483 men were wounded. 88 of the 40th were killed or died of their wounds, and about 200 were wounded. At first light on the morning of the 7 April the wounded were evacuated from the breaches, after which the dead were identified and buried.

CHAPTER 15

1. From Badajoz, Elvas is about 10 miles and Estremoz about 30 miles away.

2. This may have been Captain Phillips, who was wounded at Badajoz.

3. The Convent of San Francisco.

4. The 40th were mustered at Villa de Ciervo, on the frontier with Portugal, on 24 Dec

1812. They marched to Cedavim and were there until March.

5. This probably occurred at Cedavim in Feb 1813 after the arrival of a detachment of 5 sergeants and 144 men from the 2nd battalion.

6. ie Cedavim.

7. In March, the 40th left Cedavim and moved to Matta de Lobos where another detachment of 2 sergeants and 44 men from the 2nd battalion helped to bring the regiment up to strength.

8. Lt Kelly.

9. This incident must have happened in March 1813. It was the subject of a correspondence between General Cole, commander of the 4th Division, and the Duke of Wellington. Wellington, not realising that Kelly had married the girl, ordered her to be sent home provided she was not put into a convent. In a letter dated 26 March 1813 General Cole, informing Wellington that Kelly and the girl had been married by a chaplain, asked whether she should still be given back to her mother? (Longford p304) It is clear from Lawrence's account that the affair ended amicably.

CHAPTER 16

1. Major James Mill of the 40th, wrote letters home. Smythies quotes from them in his *History of the 40th Regt*. On 10 May, writing from Matta de Lobos, Mill says 'the *matériel* of the army has been greatly added to in the way of an extensive pontoon train, newly-constructed carts for the commissariat, and a number of Government mules provided. Captain Downs and myself have been preparing for the campaign. We have got a tent for ourselves, which we are obliged to carry on our own animals. The men's tents (3 only allowed to each company) are conveyed on Government mules. Our regiment is in a particularly healthy condition at present'.

2. 18 May 1813.

3. In boats.

4. On 30 June, Mill described the 'privations and fatigues' as 'extreme': '1½lbs of bread was the whole that was issued in 7 days previous to the battle (of Vitoria). Had it not been for a supply of horse-beans, which we gathered in the fields, we could not have gone through the protracted fatigue'.

5. Joseph Bonaparte's tactics were more defensive than those of Soult, his predecessor. Wellington's advance through Spain in pursuit of him was relentless, but at Vitoria, the French made a stand. Joseph Bonaparte had 57,000 men, Wellington 78,000.

6. General W Anson? Anson commanded the brigade to which the 40th was attached.

7. Major Mill describes how the men in his brigade advanced, in 2 lines, one 50 yards behind the other, the 40th forming the second line. The pattern of the battle - the French forming on suitable ground, being attacked, and then retiring - was repeated until 'night favoured their flight'. The distance covered that day was about 8 miles.

8. At 5pm a rumour had run through the French army that Joseph Bonaparte had ordered a general retreat: their disciplined resistance collapsed and they all converged on the road to Pamplona to try to escape. Major Mill: 'the different roads behind Vitoria were blocked with wagons and carriages of every kind, which

conveyed not only equipment and necessaries for the French soldiers, but all the worldly possessions of private individuals, of fugitives from Joseph Bonaparte's Court'. He encountered 20 wagons full of baggage and provisions from which he snatched a loaf and a piece of bacon before going on with the regiment. Others, he says, stayed behind and 'got much money'. The French Army had been paid just before the battle therefore there was money around on the battlefield for those who tarried to collect it. Wellington might have captured Joseph and his army after Vitoria had not his soldiers - and many of his officers - been so intent on capturing their loot instead.

9.   Joseph Bonaparte.
10.   The man who eloped with the Portuguese General's daughter.

CHAPTER 17

1.   In relating the events which took place in the Pyrenees between July 1813 and January 1814, William Lawrence was unable to recall the sequence exactly. With the evidence now available, it has been possible to clarify his account. However, it has not been possible to untangle it completely

2.   The regiment was mustered near Pamplona on 24 June 1813 and put to work constructing earthworks in preparation for a blockade. They were there until at least the 30 June. Their work was handed over to the Spanish and the 40th continued their march with the rest of the army towards the passes at Maya and Roncesvalles where they took up a position on the French side of the border.

3.   This may have happened near Pamplona, or at one of the other places the 40th encamped between June and November 1813.

4.   At Roncesvalles, 20 miles from Pamplona.

5.   This engagement probably happened on 25-26 July when Cole's 4th Division, unsuccessfully defending their position in the pass at Roncesvalles, retreated back towards Pamplona. In the 1886 edition, Lawrence talks about encamping for a week, but that cannot have happened, at least not at this stage in the campaign, for there was no let up in the action between 25 July and 2 August.

6.   On 26-27 July, the 3rd and 4th Divisions fell back to within 10 miles of Pamplona and took up a position on a line of hills which overlooked the valley of Zubiri down which they had retreated from Roncesvalles. Wellington, learning that his army in the Pyrenees was in retreat hurried from Lesaca to take personal charge. On 27 July he ordered two Spanish regiments, and the 40th, to occupy the summit of a rocky hill near the village of Sorauren. It was the key to the Allied position, and the action which took place there is usually identified by that name.

7.   Near Sorauren. Due to previous losses, the strength of the 40th had been reduced to 1 captain, 9 subalterns, and less than 400 men. Throughout the night of the 27th they withstood the continuous fire of 4 small guns. At 10am the next morning, the enemy attacked in force with several thousand men.

8.   Captain Sempronius Stretton who, due to casualties among the more senior officers, was commanding the regiment that day.

9.   One was Major James Mill, in charge of the 7th Company.

10.   Major James Mill gives this account: 'When the French had gained the brow of the hill, the order to charge was given, and with a threatening shout, vehement and prolonged, our battalion fell singly upon them with the bayonet, shivering their compact order and sweeping them some distance down the descent. Our men were hardly restrained from following too far, and reluctantly obeyed the orders of their officers to return to the hill.' (Smythies p147).

11.   In Maxwell's *Life of Wellington*, it is reported that the 40th fought alone for only a few minutes before a Portuguese regiment rushed up to replace the Spanish who had decamped. (Smythies, p149)

12.   In Feb 1840, in a letter to Colburn's *United Service Journal*, Stretton is as generous in his praise of the men under his command. He received a medal for this action and was promoted brevet major.

13.   Between 25 July and 2 Aug, the 40th were to lose 2 lieutenants, 3 sergeants, 35 men killed, and 150 wounded, including Lt Kelly.

14.   29 July, which Mill described as a day of perfect rest and melancholy duties, occupied as it was in burying the dead.

15.   According to Major Mill, the force which was attacked had consisted of about 2000 French.

CHAPTER 18

1.   This may have been Lt-Col Henry Thornton who took over command of the 40th on 31 Aug 1813.

2.   Sergeant Edward Ryan.

3.   The Casualty Returns for the 40th Regiment state that Ryan had been a labourer before joining the army, and that he died of wounds on 29 Nov 1813.

4.   The roll of officers of 1809 lists 2 surgeons (Meade and Wood), and 4 assistant surgeons (Bremner, Forcade, Carton and Loane). Boutflower rejoined the regiment in 1810, so it could have been him.

5.   From 24 Aug, the 40th were encamped at Lesaca in Spain, Wellington's HQ, about 15 miles west of San Sebastian, where they remained until early Sept when they moved to Echalar, also in Spain.

6.   Each regiment was ordered to supply a detachment of 1 subaltern, 1 sergeant, and 11 men, to form a forlorn hope for the storming of San Sebastian, which commenced on 31 Aug.

7.   Lawrence appears to have been misinformed. Smythies records that it was such a bloody affair only 3 of the men were unscathed. Lt Turton was so severely wounded that he died, 3 privates were killed, and the sergeant and 5 others severely wounded.

CHAPTER 19

1.   The French centre had advanced to the village of Sare, with their flanks at Espelette

and Urrugne. The 4th Div were formed up at the foot of La Rhune.

2.   The French casualties were heavy. 50 pieces of cannon and 1400 prisoners were
       taken. Lt-Col Thornton and Capts Barnett and Bishop of the 40th were wounded,
       along with about 100 of their soldiers. A sergeant and 17 rank and file were killed.

3.   The 40th were quartered in the French village of Ascain, which had earlier been
       plundered by Spanish soldiers. They were there until 8 Dec when Wellington moved
       them forward to a position between the Nive and the Adour.

4.   This engagement was on 18 Dec and is known as the Battle of the Nive. The 4th Div's
       task was to make harassing marches to the points being attacked by the French. At
       the end of December they were back in cantonments, this time in the village of
       Arrauntz.

5.   The captain may have been Stretton, but was more probably John H Barnett, who
       commanded Lawrence's company and who was wounded on the Nivelle on 10 Nov.
       As the records state that Ryan died of wounds on 29 Nov, it is possible that Lawrence
       was promoted in his place in early December, before the Battle of the Nive, while
       the regiment was at Ascain.

6.   On 3 Jan 1814. At the time the 40th had less than 450 men fit for duty.

7.   They returned to Arrauntz but were moved almost immediately to Usteritz where
       they were mustered on 24 Jan 1814.

8.   During the early months of 1814 the rain was severe and hindered operations.
       Wellington informed an impatient British Cabinet that moving troops during a
       violent fall of rain could not be done.

9.   Probably Barnett.

10.   This may have been Vera in Spain between 9 Oct and 9 Nov, or Ascain in France
       between 11 Nov and 8 Dec, or Arrauntz at the end of December. It is impossible to
       be sure.

CHAPTER 20

1.   Possibly Bidache.

2.   Major Mill said the ground they marched over was white with frost and they had to
       cross two streams by wading up to their waists in the freezing water.

3.   The figure of 5100 is too high. A regimental summary for the Peninsular War states
       that 997 sergeants, drummers and rank and file soldiers disembarked in Portugal in
       1808, and that replacements for those killed and wounded totalled 1345, giving a
       maximum of 2342, half Lawrence's figure. The strength of the regiment when it left
       France in June 1814 was 681.

4.   As soon as the war was carried into France, there were discipline problems in the
       Allied army. Some of the Spanish troops lost no time in revenging themselves for
       French atrocities in Spain by pillaging French villages, Ascain being a casualty.
       Wellington, determined not to provoke the French civilian population into taking
       up arms against him as the Spanish had taken up arms against Napoleon, decided
       on strong measures, which included sending most of the Spanish troops home.
       (Longford)

5. This was the battle for Orthez and it took place on 27 Feb 1814. The 40th took only a small part in the attack and therefore sustained few casualties.

6. Major Mill: 'Crossed the Garonne two leagues below Toulouse on the 4th. On 8 April (Good Friday) I was present with the grenadier company in supporting the attack on the bridge of Croix d'Orade. Barnett commands the grenadiers, Butler and myself are his subalterns. We were despatched down to the waterside, and lined the banks of the stream, from which position we maintained a sharp fusilade and check on the enemy, which consisted of mixed infantry and cavalry'.

7. 10 April 1814.

8. Major Mill says the shot devastated the ranks of the regiment: 'To this fire there was no reply, no rejoinder of a similar kind from our side, excepting in the way of a shout of menace and defiance from the regiment when one or more men together were stricken down by this severe fire.'

9. William Marsh did not die at Toulouse. For almost a year afterwards his name appears in the regimental muster book as being 'sick'. He was eventually discharged but, apparently, without a pension.

10. The losses of the 40th were 15 killed, 6 officers (including Captain Barnett), and 76 men wounded. The battle for Toulouse was a close run thing.

11. Soon after Wellington entered Toulouse, it was learned Napoleon had abdicated several days before on 6 April, and that Louis XVIII has been restored to the throne of France. Hostilities ended officially on 18 April when the 40th were encamped near St Felix.

12. The 40th left St Felix for cantonments at Valance where they were mustered on 24 April 1814.

CHAPTER 21

1. The destination of the 40th was Bordeaux where they were due to embark for North America, a duty from which they were later exempted because of their long service in the Peninsula. Early in May they were at Montreal, reaching Bordeaux by the middle of the month.

2. At Blanquefort.

3. Major Mill writing from the camp on 4 June said that everything was quiet, and the people particularly civil to the English: 'One sees frequently French and English soldiers walking arm in arm together, drinking in each other's company'.

4. Barnett.

CHAPTER 22

1. The 40th - 681 men strong - were ordered to Pauillac on 9 June and there put on transports which shipped them down the river to where HMS *Sultan* was anchored. They embarked on 12 June and sailed on the 14th. The British army's camp followers - the Portuguese and Spanish women who had been the soldiers'

companions throughout the long campaign, and on whom some of the men had presumably fathered children - were left behind.

2.		They disembarked on 2 July 1814.

3.		They reached Athlone on 20 July and were reinforced by 70 men from the 2nd Battalion.

4.		Orders were received to prepare the regiment for immediate service, so they left Athlone for Mallow in October. There for about 6 weeks, they were inspected and declared healthy and fit.

5.		The object of the expedition - which at the time of sailing was unknown - was to reinforce Sir Edward Pakenham's expedition to New Orleans.

6.		On 9 Oct 1814 on the transports *Lord Wellington*, *Ajax*, and *Baring*. Lawrence was almost certainly on board the *Ajax*. Their escort was HMS *Sultan*.

7.		The accident occurred in Bear (or Bere) Haven, a narrow channel between the Beara Peninsula and Bear Island, in Bantry Bay. The *Baring* had 5 companies of the 40th aboard, including Lt Hugh Wray who wrote this account in his diary the next day: 'We, thank God, have just been saved a watery grave. At 2 o'clock this morning, on entering Bere Haven (which is extremely narrow at the entrance), our Captain wished to heave-to for a pilot; but unfortunately, he attempted it too close to the mouth of the channel, had a press of sail on, and was going at the rate of eight knots, consequently the ship would not 'wear' and went smack upon the rocks, which were tremendous. Kind Providence would befriend us, for had we remained where the ship first struck, not a soul could have been saved, as the surf would have dashed a swimmer to atoms. The vessel here lost her helm, and broke a large hole in her bottom. In about 7 minutes we felt a great shock, this was the ship being absolutely heaved off the rock, and she went right across the channel (which was narrow) and put into the only spot we could have been saved in as if steered by the best helmsman in the navy (Smythies). When it struck, it was impossible to stop the men jumping overboard so it was not known if any had drowned. On 15 Oct, Lt Grove, Agent for Transport at Cork, wrote that there was every reason to believe that no lives had been lost and that it was desertion that accounted for the men who were missing. Smythies, however, states that 4 or 5 men lost their lives.

8.		In Carlisle Bay on 14 Dec.

9.		Lt William Neilley, who also kept a diary, made this entry on 9 Jan 1815: 'The *Ajax* closed... and informed us of the death of Captain Crompton by fever. The loss of this young man is universally regretted from his amiable and interesting character. What adds to increase regret... was his having exchanged with a captain of the 2nd battalion (Downes), giving up a considerable difference for the purpose of remaining on the full pay establishment'.

10.		They arrived on 22 Dec 1814.

11.		The *Moselle* escorted the convoy from Port Royal (on 27 December) to the Mississippi.

12.		A West Indian regiment, and a black regiment recruited in Georgia.

13.		The British had erected batteries out of sugar-casks because it was impossible to erect them out of earth in the waterlogged ground edging the Mississippi (Harry Smith).

14. The soldiers were on the island from 8 Feb to 18 March. They included Harry Smith and the rest of Pakenham's army. At first they were badly supplied - Smith said the men even caught, cooked and ate young alligators! - but the situation improved when peace with the Americans was concluded.

15. Harry Smith said the makeshift ovens were his idea. The iron hoops came from barrels and when they ran out, an intelligent quartermaster - Hogan of the Fusiliers - suggested using a bank of sand as a mould, the sand being removed when the cement had set. It worked.

16. Lt Wray, writing on 3 March: 'Last night our private theatre opened. The house is made of boughs of trees and covered in with large sails belonging to the ships of war. The boxes are only one on each side of the stage for the admirals and generals, and then there are seats made of planks, which form the pit. The scenery was painted by a young man of the name of Haymes, 1st lieutenant from the *Royal Oak*, and his chief colours were pipeclay, verdigris, and ochre. The dresses were mostly made up here, and some were got from the *Royal Oak*... The performance was 'The Mayor of Garrett and the Lying Valet' which was uncommonly well done. Altogether, a person would not believe it was near so well got up if they did not see it'. Performances were given 3 times a week and, after peace was declared, American officers joined the English to view them. (Smythies)

17. *Wellington, Ajax, Plantagenet*, and *Lady Banks*. They sailed on 21 March.

18. Havannah, Cuba.

19. Lawrence confused this journey home from North America with the journey home from South America in 1807. The Regimental record book states that on 25 March, in the Gulf of Mexico, the fleet encountered a thunderstorm and that lightning struck the mainmast of the *Ajax*, ran down into the hold and exploded, killing one man and injuring several others. This is undoubtedly the incident described by Lawrence in Chapter 5. The convoy anchored off Portsmouth on 15 May 1815.

20. 18 May 1815.

CHAPTER 23

1. On 23 May.

2. The 40th were in Ghent 26 May-16 June, their duties being to furnish Louis XVIII's guard and work on fortifications. On 28 May, a detachment of 77 men from the 2nd battalion joined them. With them was Maj Arthur R Heyland who assumed command of the regiment. At 5am on 16 June they received an order to march immediately to Brussels.

3. They covered 30 miles on the first day alone and halted for only a few hours at night.

4. These regiments formed the 10th infantry Brigade attached to the 6th Division commanded by Sir Lowry Cole. The strength of the 40th before the battle was 802 men and 38 officers.

5. William Bertram.

6. Major Heyland was shot through the heart. Major Fielding Browne took command of the 40th. In a written account in 1835 he explained how 'boxes of ammunition

were placed at intervals along our rear, from about 50 to 100 paces from us, so that the men could help themselves when they required it'.

7.   Major Mill describes the cannonade as tremendous: 'Whenever there was an intermission from this fire it was to find ourselves surrounded and beset by hordes of horsemen, who were slashing and cutting at our kneeling ranks. The file-firing of our standing ranks being constant and concentrated was very effectual..., and both horse and rider were to be constantly discerned rolling over on to the plain, the remainder flying backward in disorder to their own lines in very diminished numbers, leaving the ground near and around us thickly strewed with their comrades' bodies'. It was at no small cost to the men of the 40th who retained 'untiring constancy and unshaken courage on receiving wounds of a mortal kind'.

8.   The captain who died was William Fisher who commanded the 5th company. The lieutenant who replied to Marten was almost certainly the diarist Hugh Wray: 'At the time Fisher (my captain) got hit, I was speaking to him, and I got all over his brains; his head was blown to atoms'. Capt Sempronius Stretton said that the round shot that took Fisher's head off went on to kill and wound more than 25 men of his company, 'the most destructive shot I ever witnessed during a long period of Service'. There were several Martins in the 40th at about this time, the surname being a common in Ireland where the regiment recruited so many of its men.

9.   The 40th were fighting in the centre which, by early evening, was crumbling because its losses had been so great. It was a desperate time. 'I have never yet heard of a battle in which everybody was killed,' Kincaid of the Rifle Brigade remembers thinking, 'but this seemed likely to be the exception'. Wellington reinforced the centre as best he could but had Napoleon thrown against it the reserve troops he had available, the day might have been his.

10.   At about 7.30pm.

11.   Lt Wray: 'About 8 in the evening Lord Wellington came up waving his hat and hurraing, and ordered us to charge a column that was formed to cover their retreat'.

12.   Lt Wray: 'At 9 their whole army retreated in great confusion, and then, Good God! what a scene of carnage - men, horses and carriages upset and groaning, and so thick that next morning there were *fatigue* parties out to clear the road for the heavy guns... We were so fatigued as not to be able to pass the French position, where we halted that night amongst their dead and wounded'.

13.   Kincaid witnessed this too. He says two men were involved. 'When I looked in the direction of the explosion, I saw the two poor fellows about 20 or 30 feet in the air. On falling to the ground, though lying on their backs and bellies, some extraordinary effort of nature caused by the agony of the moment, made them spring from that position 5 or 6 times, to the height of 8 or 10 feet, just as a fish does when thrown on the ground after being newly caught. It was so unlike a scene of real life that it was impossible to witness it without forgetting, for a moment, the horror of their situation. I ran to the spot along with others, and found that every stitch of clothes had been burnt off, and they were black as ink all over. They were still alive, and told us their names, otherwise we could not have recognised them, and singular enough, they were able to walk off the ground with a little support, but died shortly after.'

14. Sir Lowry Cole?

15. Lt Wray: That night, 'some of our soldiers cooked their beef-steaks in the steel cuirasses (ie the protective chestplates of the French (cavalry), which completely answered the purposes of a frying-pan'.

16. Wellington's losses in killed and wounded were 15,000; Napoleon's, 25,000, the Prussians 7,000. Captain Kincaid again: 'The usual salutation on meeting an acquaintance of another regiment after an action was to ask, who had been hit? On this occasion it was, who's alive?'

17. The 40th lost 3 officers, 7 sergeants and 42 men killed, 9 officers, 12 sergeants and 147 men wounded - A total of 221. The regiment which lost 600 men was the 27th which had only 600 to lose. Kincaid: 'The 27th Regt were lying literally dead, in square, a few yards behind us'. Lt Col Ponsonby of the Light Dragoons owed his life to one of the 40th's survivors. Lying wounded on the battlefield that night, pinned down across the legs by a dying soldier, he was plundered twice: 'An hour before midnight, I saw a man in an English uniform coming towards me. He was, I suspected, on the same errand - plundering. I spoke instantly, telling him who I was. He belonged to the 40th, took up a sword, and stood guard over me as a sentinel'.

CHAPTER 24

1. From Bavais, where they were from 22-24 June they marched towards Paris, reaching Haue on 26th. Here the French had been expected to make a stand, but the town surrendered and the regiment camped a mile outside.

2. On 7 July, the 40th was encamped in Neuilly Park, about half a mile from the gates of Paris.

3. A British squadron had blockaded Rochefort to prevent vessels leaving. Napoleon boarded the *Bellerophon* on 15 July after appealing to the British government for protection.

4. Marshal Michel Ney who, after Napoleon's abdication in 1814, was retained in the army by Louis XVIII. Sent to arrest Napoleon when he returned from Elba, he chose instead to desert to his cause, and fought for him at Waterloo during the course of which 5 horses were shot from under him. He himself was shot in the Luxembourg Gardens only 6 months later on 7 Dec 1815.

5. On 22 Sept 1815. Lt Wray describes it in his journal.

6. On 22 October. It was for the benefit of Grand Duke John of Gettingstein. The manoeuvres were designed to represent the battle of Salamanca at which Lawrence was not present.

7. In the Casualty returns for the 40th, William Bertram's name appears several times as a deserter, the occasions Lawrence recounts. His final transgression was in Oct 1818 and he was discharged in Scotland on 20 Nov 1818, along with 40 other men. It is interesting to note that only a few weeks later, the regiment was officially reduced and those then discharged assessed for a pension. If the theory behind the army's use of the lash was that it turned a bad soldier into a good one, then Bertram's experience demonstrated how flawed it was. *Nothing* would have made him a good

soldier. Tom Morris, a sergeant in the 73rd Regiment said of flogging (in *Recollections of Military Service*, 1847) that it 'invariably makes a tolerably good man bad, and a bad man even worse. Once flog a man and you degrade him for ever in his own mind, and thus take from him every incentive to good conduct'. Bertram's experience endorses Morris' view. What the young man experienced wasn't punishment but victimisation. Fortunately for future recruits Morris's view was shared by men who had the power to change the situation. George Bell was a young Ensign during the latter half of the Peninsular War. He said of flogging: 'Such punishments were inhuman and I resolved in my own mind if I ever had the chance of commanding a regiment I would act upon another principle'. He got the chance and successfully abolished the lash in his own 'gallant corps'. He became Major-General Sir George Bell and wrote his memoirs - *Rough Notes of an Old Soldier*.

8.   Most of the time they were in Paris, the regiment were in tents, but on 31 Oct they were ordered to take up quarters in St Germain, 7 miles from Paris.

9.   Until 12 December 1815.

10. The 1886 edition of Lawrence's autobiography gives Clotilde's surname as Claire, but his gravestone calls her Clairet, as do most of the St Germain Municipal Records relating to the family. Clotilde's father, Jean-Pierre Clairet, is described in the Census of 1802 as a 'jardinier', 38 years old, with a wife - Marie Catherine Duguet - and 4 children. The four were almost certainly Marie Catherine Suzanne (b.1792), Marie-Louise (born about 1796), René Jean (b.1798) and Jean-Pierre (b.1801). Another child - Rose Virginie - was born to the Clairets in 1807. The family did not originate from St Germain but probably came from Daumois, where Marie Catherine had been born. In 1815, when Clotilde met Lawrence, her father would have been about 51, and her mother 48. In the census of 1819, all the family (except Marie-Catherine and Marie-Louise/Clotilde) were living at 50, rue de Pologne, St Germain. René was a junior gardner and Jean Pierre a tailor.

11. The impression given by Lawrence is that he married Clotilde while the regiment was still in St Germain. He did not. The Regiment left on 12 Dec 1815 for the villages of La Valette and La Chapelle. Clotilde went with him, but he did not marry her until 14 April 1816 by which time they had been in the area of Cambrai - nearly 100 miles from St Germain - for 2½ months. On the marriage certificate Clotilde's name is given as Cletia Clary. She could not write so the clerk probably wrote down her name as it sounded. The two witnesses were comrades of William's in the 40th - Serg I McGloghlin and Corp William Cile. With Clotilde's family 100 miles away no wonder they weren't troubled with any wedding cake!

CHAPTER 25

1.   They arrived in the area of Cambrai about 26 Jan 1816.

2.   A move took place on 14 March.

3.   Early in 1817 a decision was made to reduce the army of occupation by 5000 men. The 40th, which had been quartered in the area of Cambrai for over a year, left on 16 March 1817, arriving at Quines on 27 March. On 17 May the Waterloo medals,

granted by the Prince Regent to every man who had served at the battle, were delivered to the regiment.

4.   The transports were called the *Editha, Friendship,* and *Lord Middleton.* The regiment embarked on 30-31 March and on 2 April 1817.

5.   The *Lord Middleton* arrived at Leith on 25 April, but the *Editha* and *Friendship* hit terrible weather and were delayed.

6.   About the middle of May.

CHAPTER 26

1.   Bryant's Piddle in the 1886 edition.

2.   Lawrence had two sisters, Elizabeth and Sally. In 1817, Elizabeth would have been 23. She had married John Ridout of Piddlehinton in 1814 and already had one daughter. Sally, who was two years younger, was unmarried. Was it Sally who greeted him?

3.   Probably Samuel 28, who never married. Henry, who was 34, may have been living locally at this time, but George certainly was not. The other brother was John. Although a John Lawrence was buried in Affpuddle in 1812, William's conversation with the old villager suggests it was not his brother.

4.   In 1817, it was called Piddletown.

5.   The Rev J L Jackson was Vicar of Affpuddle (Affpiddle) and Rector of Turnerspuddle (Toner's Piddle) from 1808 to 1824, when he resigned. He was later Rector of Church Knowle, then of Swanage. There are several references to him in John Mowlem's diary.

6.   Did they survive, I wonder?

7.   Elizabeth and John Ridout and their daughter Mary-Anne were probably local, and it is likely that William's eldest brother Henry was too. For 7 years, Henry had been a blacksmith's apprentice in Bere Regis, but he was living in Affpuddle in 1816 when his son William was christened.

8.   She was Mary Scutt. The Scutts were an Affpuddle family of long standing. George and Mary's first child Henry, was born at about the time of William's visit.

9.   A shako was the tall, black, cylindrical headdress worn by soldiers of this period.

CHAPTER 27

1.   The order from the War Office came in a letter dated 24 Oct 1818.

2.   William Lawrence's discharge papers are at the PRO Kew. He is described as being 6' tall, with brown hair, hazel eyes, a sallow complexion, and aged about 32. On 19 Jan 1819, the date of his discharge, he was in fact 28. His conduct as a soldier was 'very good'.

3.   Studland is a small hamlet on the Purbeck coast. A farming and fishing area, the population of the parish in 1804 was 348. In 1841 it was 453.

4.   Dingle was, and still is, the largest town on the Dingle Peninsula in Co Kerry, on

the west coast of Ireland. It has had a colourful history but its most recent claim to fame is that *Ryan's Daughter* was filmed there. In the 14th Cent it was a substantial port with strong trading links with France and Spain.

5. The barracks in Dingle, situated in John Street, were built in 1702. The area is still known as Barrack Height although the site is now occupied by the monastery and school of the Christian Brothers.

6. The whole of the 3rd Veteran Battalion appears to have been discharged between 19-22 June 1821

7. The total, excluding the months in Studland between service with the 40th and service with the 3rd Veteran Battalion, is nearer 15½ years. The inaccuracy is due to the fact that Lawrence concealed his true age on enlistment.

8. This is how Lawrence sums up his employment for over 20 years!

9. There is no evidence that Lawrence ran a public house before 1844, the year Studland innkeeper George Damon died. By 1845 Lawrence had taken his place, changing the name of the pub from the *New Inn* to the *Wellington Inn*. Clotilde died in 1853 but William stayed on until 1856. Some time after 1856 a real 'new inn' was built on the other side of the road, and named the *New Inn* but in about 1889 it changed its name to the *Bankes Arms* which it is still called today. The period photograph of Studland in this book was taken before 1889. It features both the old pub and the new. On the right is the *Bankes Arms* then called the *New Inn*. The cottage on the left is what used to be the *Wellington Inn*. Sadly, it has been demolished.

10. The increase was valid from 8 Jan 1856 therefore the 'kind gentleman' was almost certainly his 'late master', ie George Bankes, who died on 6 July 1856. Lawrence dictated his autobiography after July 1856 but before 2 April 1867 when he received a further increase in his pension, bringing it up to 1/6d.

BIBLIOGRAPHY

PRINTED MATERIAL

BANKES, G.N. (Ed) — *Autobiography of Sergeant William Lawrence.* (Sampson, Low, Marston, Searle & Rivington, 1886.) (Facsimile edition published by Ken Trotman, 1987)

BELL, Sir GEORGE. — *Soldier's Glory: being Rough Notes of an Old Soldier.* (Spellmount, 1991.)

BOUTFLOWER, C. — *The Journal of an Army Surgeon during the Peninsular War.* (Manchester, 1912.)

BROCKLEBANK, J. — *Affpuddle: a study compiled from written sources.* (Horace G Common, 1968.)

CHALFONT, Lord. — *Waterloo: Battle of three armies.* (Sidgwick & Jackson, London, 1979.)

DAVIES, G.J. (Ed) — *Touching Withchrafte and Sorcerye.* (Dorset Record Society, 1985.)

FITCHETT, W.H. — *Wellington's Men: soldier autobiographies.* (John Murray, 1921.)

FLETCHER, I. — *Craufurd's Light Division.* (Spellmount, 1991.)

FLETCHER, I. — *The Waters of Oblivion: the British invasion of the Rio de la Plata 1806-1807.* (Spellmount, 1991.)

FRAMPTON, Mary. — *Journal of Mary Frampton.*

HARDY, W.M. — *Old Swanage, or Purbeck Past and Present.* (1910.)

LONGFORD, E. — *Wellington: the Years of the Sword.* (Tinling & Co, 1969.) (New abridged edition published by Weidenfeld & Nicolson, 1992)

MYATT, F. — *British Sieges of the Peninsular War.* (Spellmount, 1987.)

PAGE, J.V. — *Intelligence Officer in the Peninsula: letters and diaries of Edward Charles Cocks, 1786-1812.* (Spellmount, 1986.)

SMITH, Sir HARRY. — *The Autobiography of Lt-Gen Sir Harry Smith,* edited by G C Moore Smith. (John Murray, 1902.)

SMYTHIES, RH.R. — *History of the 40th Regiment,* (1898.)

THOMPSON, W.F.K.(Ed). — *An Ensign in the Peninsular War: the letters of John Aitchison.* (Michael Joseph, 1981.)

TUC. — *The Book of the Martyrs of Tolpuddle 1834-1934.* (TUC 1934.)

MANUSCRIPT SOURCES

DORSET COUNTY RECORD OFFICE, Dorchester.
Parish Registers for Affpuddle, Studland and Swanage
Frampton Estate Archives
Bankes Estates Archives
Diary of Wynne Albert Bankes, 1840-1912

DORSET COUNTY LIBRARY, Dorchester
Dorset County Chronicle, 1834.

PUBLIC RECORD OFFICE, Kew
Archive material on the 40th Regiment, including muster and pay lists, and casualty returns.
Archives of the military campaigns in South America 1806-1808, and North America 1814-1815.

INDEX